NCEA PAPERS

THE PURPOSE OF CATHOLIC SCHOOLING

by James Michael Lee

National Catholic Educational Association
NCEA Papers, Box 667, Dayton, Ohio 45401

About the Author

James Michael Lee is Chairman of the Department of Education, the Graduate School, University of Notre Dame. He is a graduate of St. John's University, New York, where he received his Bachelor's degree, and of Columbia University, where he received his Master's and Doctor's degrees. He has taught in New York City public schools and at Seton Hall University, Hunter College, St. Joseph College (Conn.), and the University of Notre Dame, where he has been Associate Professor of Education since 1965. Dr. Lee's books include *Principles and Methods of Secondary Education,* *Seminary Education in a Time of Change* (senior contributing editor), *Guidance and Counseling in Schools* (senior author), *Readings in Guidance and Counseling* (senior contributing editor), and *Catholic Education in the Western World* (contributing editor). He has published articles in professional and popular journals such as *Catholic Educational Review, Review for Religious* and *School Executive,* and has lectured throughout the United States and in Germany.

PREFACE

At no other time have the question and questioning of the purpose of Catholic schooling been so relevant. Much of the questioning to date has been notable for its lack of clarity and logic. For this reason Dr. Lee's book is more than welcome. Parents, teachers, administrators, yes, and even students will find in these pages a valuable guide for evolving the purpose of Catholic education for today's world. There is no other task more vital to the future of the American Catholic Church and, as Dr. Lee says, "it is incumbent upon every Catholic school community—to work together as a cooperative group to hammer out this purpose."

All Catholic Americans will find this book of interest since they are, in fact, co-owners of the American Catholic school enterprise—an enterprise which is priceless. If one considers the property and operational costs alone, the monetary value is great. But when one goes further and considers the investment parents make — namely, their children — the value is inestimable.

This book analyzes the purposes of Catholic schooling both ultimate and proximate. Dr. Lee bases his work on two approaches to Catholic education, the intellectualist position and the moralist position. In a very objective manner he gives the strengths and weaknesses of each point of view, drawing his information from a range of materials from St. Thomas' *Summa* and past papal encyclicals to Vatican II's *Declaration on Christian Education* and contemporary authorities in the educational field as well as in the fields of sociology, theology, philosophy and guidance.

This book requires careful reading. It is a scholarly piece of work. The author fulfills his objective in clarifying the question before us without attempting to give any pat answers. The material is well presented and will challenge those readers who recognize the import of this vital issue. In Dr. Lee's words, "effective Catholic schooling for the decisive decades ahead demands a clear concept of the distinctive purpose of the Catholic school."

No one can come away from this book without the realization that the Catholic school system has a vital and important role to play in today's society. The time is upon us to restructure the system in terms of relevance and in a way so as to insure the optimal realization of its purpose.

James Michael Lee's book is an invaluable tool for all of us involved in this task.

Very Rev. Msgr. James C. Donohue, Ph. D.
Director, Department of Education
U. S. Catholic Conference

*Education ought to teach us how to be in love always, and
what to be in love with. The great things in history have
been done by the great lovers, by saints and men of science
and artists.*[1]

—Sir Arthur Clutton-Brock

Catholic schools in America are just about everywhere and
involve in one way or another just about every Catholic
American. Catholics are asked to give generously of their
financial means to help support Catholic schools. Catholics
are urged to send their children to Catholic schools whenever
possible—actually over five million families have one or
more of their children in Catholic schools at the present
time. Catholics are exhorted to work for state and federal
legislation which will insure equitable treatment for children
in Catholic schools.

Thus Catholic Americans, parents and nonparents alike,
have a tremendous stake in Catholic schools. The total property value of Catholic school buildings and grounds, and
the annual operational costs probably total thirteen billion
dollars. Since, for the most part, Catholic schools are sup-

ported by the contributions of the laity, including parents and nonparents, the typical Catholic American "owns" a goodly share of the American Catholic school enterprise. From the personnel point of view, Catholic parents have invested their most precious possession, their children, in Catholic educational institutions. Priests, brothers, sisters, and laymen teaching in Catholic schools invest their lives, often at considerable financial sacrifice, to teach and administer Catholic schools.

With the increasing investment of money and of personnel in American Catholic schools, and with the emergence of an intelligent laity and a sophisticated clergy, the question is being increasingly asked: "What is the purpose of the Catholic school?" Other than the broad objective "to help our children save their souls," there has never been any official binding specific purpose to direct American Catholic schools.[2] Many scholars, members of the hierarchy, and Catholic organizations have from time to time expressed their views on what they believe should be the purpose of Catholic schooling in the United States. However, with the increasing crisis in American Catholic schools due to a shortage of financial resources, to the decline in religious vocations, and to an intelligent laity, which more and more questions the validity of the Catholic school, the day is soon coming when the Church in America, both clergy and laity, must forge a clearcut official statement of specific purposes of the Catholic school. It is the goal of this book in a modest way to assist Catholic Americans to clarify their thinking on what they wish the purpose of Catholic schooling to be.

Education and Schooling

The terms "education" and "schooling" should not be taken synonymously, since there is a vast difference between the two. Education is the process whereby a person learns something. Consequently, a person is always in the process of being educated at every moment of his waking life and in a vast panoply of situations. Learning to walk or to play the piano, watching a baseball game on television, strolling along the beach, developing facility in speaking German, falling in love—these are all part of a person's education.

Schooling, then, constitutes only one segment of a person's education. Sometimes schooling is called "formal education," indicating that it is a planned, systematic, deliberate activity which has as its main objective to sharpen, enhance, and codify the educative process. As a definition, formal education is the totality of experiences which the school directly or indirectly furnishes the student to enable him to develop and mature. These experiences include intellectual learning, motor learning, appetitive learning, appreciational learning, moral conduct, social skills, emotional growth, spiritual satisfaction, and guidance.

The distinction between education and schooling might seem elemental; nonetheless it is surprising to find how frequently it is ignored by many persons, even scholars. That the difference between the two terms is an axial one can be illustrated by the following problem. "All Catholics are bound in conscience before God and the Church to provide their children with a Catholic education. However, does this necessarily imply that all Catholics are obliged to send their children to a Catholic school?" If education and schooling were identical, then the answer would be a resounding "yes." But since the terms are distinct, it becomes obvious that Catholic parents are obliged to send their children to a Catholic school *only* if such is necessary for the child's overall Catholic education. Thus a child might be able to receive a well-rounded Catholic education without ever attending a Catholic school. It is well to remember that total Catholic schools did not exist until at least the fourth century, indicating that the early Christians viewed Catholic education and Catholic schooling as distinct entities. Some contemporary Catholic Americans believe that Catholic schooling at certain school levels and for certain children might in some cases actually be injurious to the Catholic education of those children.[3] One prominent Catholic educationist has stated flatly that it is "un-Christian" for a Catholic child to receive his entire schooling under Catholic auspices.[4] Others believe that for a well-rounded Catholic education, every Catholic child should spend at least one segment of his schooling in a government school.

Catholic schooling, then, is not necessary for Catholic education. It is unfortunate that in our own era every essence, every worthwhile thing, seems to be locked into some organization. Even at a vacation resort where one goes "to get away from it all" the leisure is carefully organized by a social director. Just as it is possible for a person to have fun at a resort without participating in its organized program of activities, so also is it possible to become Catholically educated without participating in the organized program that is a Catholic school.

There is a time-tested axiom which states, "Don't neglect your education for your studies." This is particularly germane as far as Catholic education is concerned. The primary and by far the most important educative influence on the child is not his school but his family. No institution has stressed the primacy of the family in the child's education more than the Catholic Church—and for good reason. The empirical research clearly shows that the most formative period in a person's life with respect to forging his deeper attitudes, values, and beliefs, is the period from birth to six years of age. Hence the old saw: "Give me a child for his first six years and you can have him for the rest of your life." The carefully conducted large scale research investigation, undertaken by Andrew Greeley and Peter Rossi, of Catholic adults who had attended Catholic schools and those who had attended government schools indicated that the family is a vastly more significant force than is Catholic schooling in affecting the person's future religious behavior. Indeed, this study concluded that by far the most significant factor in providing Catholic education to the child is his family.[5]

It is unfortunate that in this age of emphasis on formal organizations parents tend to relegate their indispensable educative task almost totally to the school. Whether the child is in a Catholic school or in a government school, parents ought always to remember that they are the primary educational agents in the life of their child—primary by right as parents and primary by scope of impact on the education of their child. The school, whether a Catholic school or a government school, is merely supplemental to the educative influence of the parents. The school can only build on what the parents have already done educationally, and what the parents continue to do educationally while the child is simultaneously in school. This fact is not only a psychologically verified one, but it was also juridically reinforced by the United States Supreme Court in the landmark Oregon decision in 1925.[6] Julius Cardinal Döpfner of Munich expressed these same sentiments with clarity during the discussion on priestly formation at the Second Vatican Council.[7] The *Declaration on Christian Education* of Vatican II expressed this concept beautifully:

> Part of its [the State's] duty is to promote the education of the young in several ways: . . . by implementing the principle of subsidiarity and completing the task of education with attention to parental wishes, whenever the efforts of parents and of other groups are insufficient.[8]

In the light of what has been said in the preceding paragraphs, is Catholic schooling valid in the contemporary world? The present writer strongly believes it is both valid and vital. However, it goes without saying that to be valid and vital, Catholic schooling must realign both its structures and its purposes so as to be relevant for those who are attending its schools. Old structures and old purposes had their place in former times; however a Church (and its school system) which like its Founder strives to be preeminently incarnational must constantly plunge its structures and its purposes into the present moment.

The structures of schooling in terms of curricula, levels of Church-sponsored schools, emphasis on certain sectors of society, and so forth must be radicated in the purpose of that schooling. The structures are concretizations, objectifications of the basic purpose. It is to this point that this book now turns its attention.

The Catholic School as a Protest School

Once upon a time ecclesiastical officials in both Europe and the United States insisted that schooling was primarily and exclusively *the* function of the Church. Indeed, near the turn of the present century Thomas Bouquillon, a clerical professor at the Catholic University of America, was silenced by the American hierarchy because he proposed that schooling is one of the State's basic functions.[9] But in our day, while the Church still insists that providing education remains *a* primary right of the Church, it does not deny that it is also a primary right of the State.[10]

In the practical order, however, the government school constitutes the typical form of schooling for the vast majority of the nation's youth in almost all developed countries. In the United States, about 85 percent of all persons attending school attend the government school. Today, therefore, the Catholic school represents a protest school;[11] Catholic parents protest that the government is not providing the type of school which they deem essential for their children. This protest takes the concrete form of a separate Catholic school or school system.

It is precisely in this concept of a "protest school" that are found the existential seeds of the purpose of Catholic schooling. Unless the private Catholic protest school serves an educational purpose essentially distinctive from the government school, then it has no legitimate basis for existence. There are two elements in this statement. First, the Catholic school must be radically and essentially distinctive in its purpose. The foundation for this conclusion is the familiar philosophical principle of Ockham's razor: "Beings should not be multiplied without necessity." Public schools exist in abundance, and in virtually every community in the land.

New—and in one sense "competing"—schools should not be set up side by side with the public schools unless these "competing" schools are truly distinctive and essentially different. Also adduced in support of this conclusion is the hallowed principle of subsidiarity: "A being of a higher ontological order (in this case, the Church) should not perform functions which a being of a lower ontological order (in this case, the government) can perform equally well."[12] Thus if the government is providing basically the same education as the Catholic school, if the purposes of public and Catholic schools are not essentially distinct, then the Church should not operate separate schools. The second element is that the Church school must be actually fulfilling both its own distinctive purpose as well as those purposes it shares with the public school. It is outside the scope of this book to discuss this second element.

As a valid protest school, Catholic schooling aims in a general way at furnishing the student with a coherent, meaningful, and intensified form of Catholic education. The Catholic school aims at providing a deep mode of Catholic education for the student, a mode deeper and more religiously integrational than is possible in a government school or in no school at all.

In former times, when Catholic schoolmen were less sophisticated and more ghettoistic than they are in today's open Church, the epithet "those godless public schools" was hurled with great frequency. This accusation, happily, has been quietly laid to rest. Nothing in God's world is godless. Indeed, the public schools, with their often fine scholastic programs and dedicated professional staffs (many of whom are devout Catholics), do provide a Catholic education in the sense that the outcomes derived from these schools lead the student to God. Catholic schools, over and above this, have as their goal the furnishing of a richer type of Catholic education than is found in the public schools. The Catholic school attempts, among other things, to provide a conscious, well-organized, systematic integration of religion with the other aspects of the curricular and guidance programs. It is this saliency, this deliberately structured integration which constitutes one of the primary distinctions between the government and the Catholic schools.

Types of Purpose

There is no single exclusive purpose underlying Catholic schooling; rather, any given Catholic school incorporates several types of purposes at the same time. This is not to imply that Catholic schooling in general or one Catholic school in particular is a maze of conflicting purposes. Rather, there are various orders and kinds of purposes operative in any one particular school.

It would be a grave mistake to regard the purpose of Catholic schooling as merely some official but irrelevant statement issued by a pastor or a bishop. On the contrary, the purpose of Catholic schooling is terribly important. It bristles with relevancy. After all, the purpose of Catholic schooling is the very cause of the founding of that type of schooling. Further, the distinctive purpose of Catholic schooling is precisely why parents choose to send their children to a Catholic educational institution. The purpose of the school is the first and most important reason both for the existence of the school and for the motivation of parents to send their children to that school. In formal Scholastic terminology, "although purpose is last in the order of the person's actually doing something, nonetheless it is the very first in the order of his intention to do it. In this way the purpose is a cause."[13] If either the purpose does not exist in a parent's intention to send his child to a Catholic school, or if the purpose is not clearly focused, then the very outcomes which are expected from that school will go unfilled. Consequently it is crucial for Catholic educators, for parents, for other members of the People of God, and particularly for the students to have a clear concept of the various purposes of the Catholic school with which they are most closely affiliated.

To a very great degree, the purpose of a school will have

a large conditioning effect on which specific means are used to bring about learning in that school. For example, if the purpose of one kind of secondary school is to serve as a private "finishing school" for Catholic young ladies, the specific means employed in that school (e.g., teaching methods, curriculum, school building, and so on) will be quite different from those of another type of Catholic secondary school whose purpose is to have its graduates enter high-powered universities. To a certain extent, the purpose not only tends to specify the means, but even more, tends to contain in seed many of the means. As will be seen later, Catholic schools are widely divergent in some of their most fundamental specific purposes; consequently the means, the emphasis in these schools, will differ considerably. It is incumbent on the Catholic parent and child, therefore, to make careful inquiry into the precise purpose of the particular school so as to insure that what will be learned in that school conforms to the basic reason for the parent sending the child there.

The first broad type of purpose is that of *ultimate purpose.* The ultimate purpose of Catholic schooling is that purpose to which all other purposes are subordinated and which itself is not subordinated to any other purpose or goal.[14] The ultimate purpose is consequently a broad and general purpose [15] to which everything in the school program is somehow in an overall way ordered. The ultimate purpose is not some deferred goal in the misty future. Rather, it is very much present in a general, pervasive, teleological way in every aspect of the school program. As to the future, the ultimate purpose of Catholic schooling constitutes the most important general outcome which the student carries with him for the rest of his life.

The second broad type of purpose is that of *proximate purpose.* The proximate purpose of Catholic schooling is that outcome which, although immediate, is also intended to be operative throughout the student's life. The proximate purpose constitutes one specific, distinctive purpose within the broad general ken of the ultimate purpose. Whereas the ultimate purpose of a Catholic school can be attained by use of a wide variety of means, the proximate purpose demands a far more restricted range of means, indeed often only one single set of means. Hence, while the ultimate purpose constitutes the goal which most distinguishes Catholic schooling from government schooling, it is the proximate purpose which principally distinguishes one Catholic school from another Catholic school.

Within the category of proximate purpose there are the primary proximate purpose and the secondary proximate purpose. The primary proximate purpose is the most important specific goal which the school hopes to achieve as a direct and immediate result of the educational program conducted there. The secondary proximate purpose is any concomitant outcome which, although important, is nonetheless subordinate to the primary proximate purpose. While a school has only one primary proximate purpose, it concomitantly has several secondary proximate purposes.

The third broad type of purpose is that of the *level of school*. Thus each school level, viz., kindergarten, elementary, secondary, undergraduate university, and graduate university, does not have the same kind of purpose. This type of purpose, however, is more relevant to the proximate purpose than to the ultimate purpose since, in theory at least, all Catholic educational institutions do have the same ultimate purpose.

It is quite important to keep in mind that a purpose is not something which is completely rigid or is absolutely fixed. Both progressive educationists in America and existentialist philosophers in Europe have demonstrated that a totally fixed and rigid end (other than God Himself, of course) is not true to life, and indeed squeezes out life. To regard a purpose as something which inexorably causes one and only one specific set of means is, as John Dewey pointed out, quite "mechanistic."[16] Further, the purpose of Catholic schooling is not simply a product outcome, but also (and perhaps more importantly) a process outcome. Surely for the archer to hit the mark (product outcome) is important; however, the hitting of the mark (process outcome) is also of vital importance. To be able to obtain the number 638 as the product of multiplying 22 and 29 is important, to be sure, but of great (and probably of greater) importance is to acquire the process skill of multiplying these two numbers. Process outcomes are less tangible than product outcomes, yet usually they are more enduring and more productive of realizing the basic purposes of the Catholic school.

There is one very basic problem concerning this entire matter of purposes. Simply stated, this problem is as follows: is the purpose of the Catholic school the same as the purpose of the child who is attending that school? If these purposes are different, then truly the stated or the real purpose of the Catholic school, as school officials perceive it, is nothing more than empty phrases. To be real, the purpose of the school must be both perceived and lived by every student. After all, it is the student's purpose which is the real purpose; in terms of what he will learn in the school, it is in the long run the only purpose which really matters.

The Ultimate Purpose of Catholic Schooling

Virtually every Catholic educator agrees on the ultimate purpose of Catholic schooling. Bishop Ernest Primeau stated this purpose very well when he spelled it out as "the formation of a people acceptable to God. And the people will be acceptable to God when they know, love, and serve Him and know, love, and serve one another in Him."[17]

It is this ultimate purpose which makes Catholic schools and government schools essentially distinct in terms of basic aims. It would, however, be a grave mistake to think that this basic distinction between government and Catholic schools, while essential, is also exclusive. It was demonstrated earlier in this book that government schools are not godless or devoid of Christian values. The educational program of government schools indirectly and indeed often directly leads the student toward a deeper religious life. The psychologist Jung once

noted: "Called or not, God is present."[18] Nonetheless, the formal ultimate purpose (to use philosophical terminology) of the government school is citizenship formation, not religious formation. Naturally such a worthy purpose, far from excluding religious formation, of its very nature includes it. On the other hand, religious formation is precisely the ultimate *raison d'être* of the Catholic school. Since the ultimate purpose of an institution gives the basic (but not, of course, the total) guidelines and thrust to a school's educational program, the Catholic school is radically distinct from the government school because it is consciously structured to produce religious outcomes. It is this deliberate structure based on the ultimate goal which basically distinguishes Catholic schools from government schools. The overt orientation between the two school systems, therefore, is formally and actually distinct.

The ultimate purpose of Catholic schooling clearly is too general to make it an institution distinctive from other forms of the apostolate within the institutional Church. In the words of Neil McCluskey, S.J.: "It fails to indicate the specific objective, that which distinguishes the school *as such* from the hospital, the retreat house, the parish, or the foreign mission."[19] Each of these institutions has as its ultimate purpose religious formation and the saving of souls. Thus, while the ultimate purpose makes Catholic schools essentially distinct from non-Catholic schools, it is the primary proximate purpose which makes the Catholic school qua school essentially distinct from other agencies of the Church.

The Primary Proximate Purpose of Catholic Schooling

There is substantial and often heated disagreement among Catholic educators and educationists on what constitutes the primary proximate purpose of the Catholic school. Although the popes and the bishops have indeed spoken their views on what they believe is the primary proximate goal of the Catholic school, nonetheless there is no "official" position in the sense of binding Catholic educators under faith or morals. Hence, Catholics not only are free to debate this issue, but in point of fact have deliberately established schools based on one or other primary proximate goal. The primary proximate purpose of the school is often shortened in everyday speech to simply "the purpose of the school." Because this question of purpose is so important in the lives of so many contemporary Catholics, the remainder of this book will be allotted to a careful examination of this question.

In general, three positions have been enunciated on the primary proximate purpose of the Catholic school: the moralist, the intellectualist, and the integralist. Each of these will be discussed in the pages which follow. Before entering into this, however, several points should be borne in mind relevant to the treatment of this thorny and difficult problem. For all but a very few educators, "primary" is not to be equated with "exclusive." Thus, for example, an intellectualist might readily admit that the moral development of the child is one of the secondary purposes of the Catholic school, co-existing with the more basic and primary purpose for the Catholic school's existence. The second point to be remembered is that any abstract, generalized division of views, while essentially valid, nonetheless in one sense does not completely represent each position in its fullness or with the living nuances which characterize the dynamics of each view. Third, while in theory various Catholic schoolpeople ardently embrace one or other of the opposing views, in actual practice their own educational work in the classroom not infrequently deviates from what they maintain in their theoretical position. Hence, if a parent or other member of the People of God sincerely wishes to ascertain the real goal of the school, he ought to examine what actually goes on there rather than merely listen to the statements of schoolpeople about what is supposed to go on there. Finally, the viewpoints of many scholars and prominent personages will be treated. These viewpoints are not being presented in an effort to maneuver or even subdue the reader into one or other conclusion, for as Thomas Aquinas himself observed, arguments based on human authority are the weakest of all arguments.[20] Rather, contrasting views are presented so that, with the opinions of men who have given great thought to this matter, the reader may the better decide for himself what is or what should be the primary proximate purpose of the Catholic school with which he is the most closely associated.

The Moralist Position

Those parents, students, and teachers who hold the moralist position believe that the primary proximate purpose of the Catholic school is directly to bring the students closer to Christ. This approach has been the traditional one in American Catholic schools. Although its heyday was in the century from 1850 to 1950, it still is very widely held today. In fact, it is probably the position held by the majority of those teaching in American Catholic elementary and secondary schools, and of the religious teaching in Catholic women's colleges.[21]

There are sound, solid reasons why the moralist position is firmly rooted in the soil of the history of American Catholicism. Public schools in the United States until at least the turn of the 20th century were in many ways Protestant schools. Consequently, to preserve the faith of their children, Catholic American parents and clergy were led to erect their own separate schools. Further, from colonial days until well into the 20th century, there has been a vocal and not infrequently powerful strain of anti-Catholicism in American life. Prior to the Revolutionary War, Catholics were directly or indirectly persecuted in practically every colony with the exception of Pennsylvania. Anti-Catholic feeling in the United States reached its zenith in the mid-19th century in the deep-seated and pervasive movement known as Nativism. Even in the 20th century, latent anti-Catholic feelings in the United States were clearly brought into the open in the 1928 presidential campaign.

Another firm historical reason explaining the moralist posture in American Catholic education is found in the fact that members of French religious institutes, particularly women's institutes, played a predominant role in the establishment of early American Catholic schools. Not a few of these French religious institutes were influenced quite heavily by Jansenism, a 17th century French heresy whose tone was at once pietistic and anti-intellectualistic. In addition, the then contemporary exemplars of Catholic schooling in France tended to be moralistic. The little school established by the Curé of Ars to train girls in home economics nicely illustrates this point, claims Kevin O'Brien, C.S.S.R., a staunch defender of the moralist position.[22] O'Brien notes that "there can be no doubt that the emphasis of the school was on the formation in true piety. (With the holy Curé as chaplain, could it be otherwise?)." O'Brien concedes that "the standard of intellectual formation given these girls of 12 to 18 would shock the intellectuals." Further, the school building was dilapidated and overcrowded to double capacity. There was only one classroom, 18 feet by 8 feet, with all the classes going on at once. In conclusion, O'Brien observes that in an official decree, Pope St. Pius X called this school a "model of popular education."

Advocates of the moralist position are careful to point out that papal statements have consistently underscored the fact that the primary proximate purpose of Catholic schooling is moralistic. In these statements the popes do not say that development of the student's spiritual life is the exclusive primary proximate purpose. What the popes do maintain is that all the Catholic school activities, including their academic studies, are but means to the student's moral formation. Religious instruction, the religious "atmosphere" of the school, the academic curricula are all paths toward fulfilling the specific and immediate goal of the school, viz., the development of personal sanctity.

Some representative papal statements will serve to illustrate this point. Pius XII, in an allocution to teaching sisters, stated:

According to the Catholic concept, the object of the school and of education is the formation of the perfect Christian . . . Your entire school and educational system would be useless were this object not the central point of your labor.[23]

In his message to the Fifth Inter-American Congress on Catholic Education, this same pontiff wrote:

Good teachers, finally, are careful to educate rather than merely to instruct; capable above all of forming and molding souls . . . You will interest yourselves more in education than in mere instruction.[24]

The text of this address, while leading to the interpretation that such molding might go on in classrooms, also appears to indicate that such molding occurs in the nonclass school activities, and in postgraduation follow-up activities. Nonetheless, it would seem that all these in-school and out-of-school activities are conceived in the papal mind as constituting the primary proximate purpose of the Catholic school.

In a letter to the bishops of Czechoslovakia, Pius XI wrote:

Therefore, Venerable Brethren, do not tire of insistently warning Catholic parents that it is their serious duty to train their children in holiness and they have the right from natural law to found Catholic schools or to demand, according to their means, that even in the public schools the faith of their children be preserved from all dangers, and that their minds and wills be formed according to the rules of Christianity.[25]

Undoubtedly the most frequently quoted papal text is the famous 1929 encyclical on Christian education, *Divini Illius Magistri:* "The proper and immediate aim of Christian education is to cooperate with divine grace in forming the true and perfect Christian, that is to form Christ Himself in those regenerated by Baptism."[26] Parents and Catholic educators who uphold the moralist position have indicated that this text is the Magna Carta of their position. Opponents, on the other hand, claim that the pope was talking here not of the primary proximate end of the Catholic school but rather of Catholic education in general. However, a careful examination of the context of the pope's remarks would seem to indicate that the pontiff is indeed speaking specifically of the Catholic school and not of Catholic education in general. To be sure, his remarks come at the culmination of an eight-page treatment of the Catholic school.[27]

Pius XI, while indicating that the primary proximate aim of the school is moral-religious, does not make this the exclusive goal. Rather, the other areas of the school are viewed as vital and helpful means toward the realization of this purpose. In the paragraph immediately following the above-quoted text, Pius continues:

... Christian education takes in the whole of human life, physical and spiritual, intellectual and moral, individual, domestic and social, not with a view to minimizing it in any way, but in order to elevate, regulate, and perfect it, in accordance with the example and teaching of Christ.[28]

Again the context makes it clear that Pius is referring to Catholic schools, even though he uses the word "education."

While stressing the necessity of strong intellectual training in schools as one means of "forming the true and perfect Christian," Pius nevertheless leaves no doubt that intellectual formation has no autonomy, but in all things must be ordered by and regulated unto the fundaments of moral-religious formation. Thus, in describing what he conceives to be the model Catholic school, the pontiff writes:

And if, when the occasion arises, it be deemed necessary to have the students read authors propounding false doctrine, for the purpose of refuting it, this will be done after due preparation and with such an antidote of sound doctrine, that it will not only do no harm, but will be an aid to the Christian formation of youth.[29]

Some Catholic educators and parents opposed to the moralist position believe that while perhaps the pope was here speaking of the Catholic elementary schools, he was probably excluding Catholic secondary schools and certainly not including Catholic institutions of higher learning. However, precisely the opposite is true. The pope specifically included Catholic schools at all levels, as can easily be seen from the following passage from the same encyclical:

> The mere fact that a school gives some religious instruction (often extremely stinted), does not bring it into line with the rights of the Church and of the Christian family, or make it a fit place for Catholic students. To be this, it is necessary that all the teaching and the whole organization of the school, its teachers, syllabus and textbooks of every kind, be regulated by the Christian spirit, under the direction and maternal supervision of the Church; so that religion may be in very truth the foundation and crown of the youth's entire training; and this applies to every grade of school, not only the elementary, but the intermediate and the higher institutions of learning as well. To use the words of Leo XIII, "It is necessary not only that religious instruction be given to the young at certain fixed times, but also that every other subject taught be permeated with Christian piety. If this is wanting, if this sacred atmosphere does not pervade and warm the hearts of masters and scholars alike, little good can be expected from any kind of learning, and considerable harm will often be the consequence."[30]

Certainly another powerful factor in causing the moralist position to be espoused by so many Catholic teachers and school administrators is the fact that many of the most influential Catholic writers on education were staunch adherents of the moralist position. This is not to imply that all the Catholic educational writers over the past 40 years were moralists. To be sure, many of these Catholic authors such as William Cunningham and William McGucken were opponents of this position. Nonetheless it is fair to say that the majority of the more influential Catholic educational writers were moralists. The writings of a large percentage of the teaching sisters and brothers, and of a substantial number of priests engaged in Catholic school work reflects a decided moralist bent as to the purpose of the Catholic school. Further, the two most influential textbooks used in education courses at Catholic universities, viz., those of Franz de Hovre and of John Redden and Francis Ryan, were stout defenders of the moralist position. Since those of the teaching sisters, brothers, priests, and laymen who did receive university preparation in education studied from these textbooks, a definite formative influence was exerted on these schoolmen.

Perhaps the most influential textbook on education used in Catholic institutions of higher learning in the mid- and late 1930s was *Catholicism in Education*, by Franz de Hovre. Of the primary proximate purpose of Catholic schools, de Hovre writes:

> Education deals with the soul of man; its object is his complete transformation from a child of the flesh to a child of God. It aims to open his mind to the vision of the truth, to clarify his sense of values, to adjust him to the things of eternity as well as the things of time, to make him a faithful member of the divine society which Christ established, to lead him to God . . . Education is an ethical, a religious activity which is concerned with things that rank highest in the scale of values: the soul of the child and its eternal destiny, the truths of Christianity, the Church, and God.[31]

It is quite clear from the context of both the book and the passage that de Hovre, while employing the word "education," clearly meant "the school."

From the early 1940s until the early 1960s surely the most influential Catholic textbook in education was *A Catholic Philosophy of Education*, by John Redden and Francis Ryan. The distinctive characteristic of Catholic schools, contended Redden and Ryan, is the centering of the entire educative process around religion. Religion is the core; all other subjects of the curriculum are integrally related to and revolve around it. These secular subjects of the curriculum, with their own properly recognized aims and objectives, should be given due emphasis to insure their respective contributions to the immediate and ultimate aims of education, both from the individual and the social standpoints. In such emphasis, however, it should be recognized that these subjects must always be taught as means to ends.[32]

Like de Hovre, Redden and Ryan go to considerable effort in their attempt to refute opponents of their position, such as John Henry Cardinal Newman and William Cunningham.[33]

Many teaching religious in their own personal and professional lives have been heavily influenced by the educational writings either of their founder(ress) or of some key person in their institute who wrote an educational tract. Most of these persons rather strongly championed the moralist position as a guideline for the purpose of their institute entering school work. Thus the writings of Jean Baptiste de la Salle, the 17th century founder of the Brothers of the Christian Schools, are well known in this regard. A representative example of the second type, i.e., the writings of a key non-founder(ress) of a religious institute, is contained in a rather lengthy book authored by Sister Barbara Zulinska. This volume, appropriately entitled *Ad Resurrectionem,* "is an integration of the educational principles which guide the work of the Congregation of the Resurrection,"[34] a female religious institute founded near the beginning of the present century. The following quotations illustrate the moralist conception of the school's primary proximate purpose:

Catholic education, therefore, is the tracing of the work of the Holy Spirit in each soul, facilitating the following of the voice of inspiration at every moment of life, guiding the process of spiritual development.[35]

> Pedagogy is the science which is based on ethics,
> because it teaches how to impart the skill to act to
> those faculties which take part in moral actions.[36]
> [One of the] fundamental principles of Catholic
> pedagogy is to "infuse a humility of the mind so
> that knowledge will not become harmful."[37]

It should be noted that in context, the word "education" in
the passages quoted above clearly means "school."

Support for the moralist view of the Catholic school's
primary proximate purpose also came from a significant
percentage of bishops and clergy who were not directly con-
nected with school work as such. Thus, for example, Msgr.
George A. Kelly, who until the mid-1960s was a New York
chancery official originally specializing in marriage-family
life, and a member of a former Papal Commission studying
birth control, wrote in his *The Catholic Family Handbook*
that "moral teaching should hold first place in the classroom."[38] Moral teaching here implies not only instruction in
religious truths, but also the active encouragement of living
a spiritual life. Kelly maintains that the superior school is
not the one with the best overall scholastic achievement but
the one which most effectively teaches the pupil the Christian position in his "relationship to his Creator, his fellow-
man and nature."[39]

By the time the mid-1960s had rolled around, more and
more Catholic theorists on education had begun to voice
opposition openly to the moralist position. These men represent an impressive array of names, including Neil G. Mc-
Cluskey, John Tracy Ellis, Thomas T. McAvoy, Leo R. Ward,
and Herbert Johnston, to name but a few. While it is difficult
to state with certainty whether or not the anti-moralist position represents the view of the majority of the new theorists,
one can nonetheless say that there is a strong trend in this
direction.

Yet the moralists still have their champions. One of the
most vigorous of these is Kevin O'Brien, whose 1958 book

is perhaps the most comprehensive defense of this position. O'Brien notes that the primary proximate purpose of the Catholic school at all levels is to teach the students to "do all for the love of God."[40] Secular knowledge, he holds, is not very important anyway. Indeed, "knowledge without moral formation is simply a weapon in the hands of a criminal."[41] O'Brien maintains that the world should not worry so much about educating a poor, devout, but intellectually backward savage in some distant land, because "he has in his will charity which is superior to all knowledge in this life."[42] To be sure, even the best natural knowledge ignores reality.[43] All else except development of a rich spiritual life counts for little in Catholic schooling. In his words: "It is surely an anomaly to have Catholic high school children coming each day to school and seldom if ever making a voluntary visit to the Blessed Sacrament in the church nearby."[44]

Thus far, this treatment has presented exclusively the thoughts of influential Catholic officials and theorists on the primary proximate goal of Catholic schools. But what is the reality in practice? In actual fact, why do parents send their children to Catholic schools? And what do students in Catholic schools perceive as the primary proximate aim of their school? Fortunately, there have been two extensive research investigations which clearly provide hard data by way of answering this question. The conclusion of both studies is that Catholic parents perceive the primary proximate purpose of Catholic schools as moralist.

Perhaps the most comprehensive research investigation into the status of the American Catholic educational enterprise was conducted by Reginald Neuwien and associates.[45] Neuwien's study concluded that in the opinion both of parents of the children in Catholic elementary and secondary schools as well as of the children themselves, the primary proximate purpose of Catholic schooling is moral-religious.[46] Neuwien's study embraced a carefully selected but relatively large and representative sampling of Catholic elementary and secondary school children throughout the United States.[47] His research

instrument gave each student five alternatives from which to choose his own most important personal goal for his Catholic schooling. The percentages, as they fell in each of the choice areas, were: (1) moral-religious, 60.5; (2) occupational-vocational, 14.3; (3) intellectual-academic, 12.5; (4) friendship-social, 6.4; (5) civic-patriotic, 6.0.[48] Predictably, the parents of these children indicated that they also believed that the primary proximate goal of the Catholic school is in the moral-religious cluster.[49]

A complementary, and in some respects, a companion investigation undertaken by Andrew Greeley and Peter Rossi came to substantially the same conclusion.[50] Greeley and Rossi studied two groups of adult Catholics: a selected group of average, representative Catholics, and a group of Catholics identified by the researchers as being "intellectual and liberal elite."[51] In the first group, i.e., the average Catholic American, 73 percent of the respondents believed that "religious instruction" was the principal advantage of Catholic schooling. The next highest category chosen was "better discipline," with 38 percent.[52] Interestingly, and indeed to the surprise of the researchers, the liberal and intellectual elite are more inclined than anyone else in the general sample to stress the primacy of religious training in Catholic schools. Indeed, a resounding 93 percent of *The Commonweal* respondents rated religious instruction as the principal advantage of Catholic schooling. The next category was chosen by only 29 percent of the respondents.[53]

Inasmuch as no institution in the world has stressed with greater insistence the fact that the school does and must represent the wishes of the parents with regard to the thrust of the education of their children, the findings of the Neuwien investigation and of the Greeley-Rossi study are of signal importance.

The Intellectualist Position

Those parents, students, and teachers who hold the intellectualist position believe that the primary proximate purpose of the Catholic school is the intellectual development of the student. In the words of Thomas Donlan, O.P., "the perfection of the mind through the intellectual virtues is sought as the proximate or immediate end. The distinctive means employed by the school are proper to the school and are not distinctive of any other agency of education."[54] However, as Donlan adds, to assert that the primary proximate end of the school is the inculcation of the intellectual virtues "is not to maintain that these same virtues are the principal goal of life"; rather, it is simply to assert that as far as the school's role as a distinctive agency of education is concerned, the intellectual virtues are the most important object.[55] The school does not comprise all of education; it is only one agency, one mode of education.

It is possible to distinguish within the ranks of the intellectualists two divergent groups, viz., the strict intellectualists and the moderate intellectualists. The strict intellectualists, of whom Vincent Edward Smith is perhaps a typical representative, believe that knowledge and the intellectual virtues constitute the only true and legitimate proximate purpose or outcome of the school properly considered. In this view, school is identified solely with "learning from a teacher in the strict sense and of the curriculum as the instrument of this process."[56] It is the curriculum which makes the school a distinctive and ontologically specific institution from all the other agencies of education. Further, teaching is virtually totally discursive. And since it is discursive, teaching is at its best when the syllogism, whether in complete or incomplete, form, is employed.[57] Consequently, imperfectly discursible subjects or areas of knowledge are imperfectly teachable. Drawing almost totally upon an Aristotelean and a Thomistic metaphysical analysis, Smith noted that only the intellectual disciplines can be included in the category of "teachable subjects;" hence they and they alone really belong in the school properly considered.[58] (Smith identifies these teachable subjects or disciplines to be six: logic, mathematics, natural science, moral science or ethics, metaphysics, and theology.)[59] Finally, since the school's exclusive proximate purpose is to educate in the teachable intellectual virtues, it stands to reason that it is a great fallacy for the school to attempt to educate the whole person. Such an endeavor is a fallacy precisely because the means to educate the intellect differs radically from the means used to educate other faculties and constituents of the whole person, e.g., the will, the emotions, and so forth.[60]

Parents, students, and educators who adhere to the moderate intellectualist position tend to be more subtle and supple in their reasoning than are the proponents of the strict intellectualist position. Advocates of the moderate intellectualist aim believe that knowledge and the intellectual virtues constitute the Catholic school's primary but not exclusive proximate purpose. Other and highly worthwhile purposes might operate either concomitantly or as by-products of the means toward and the outcomes of intellectual development; however, such nonintellectual purposes at best must be properly considered as secondary or tertiary proximate purposes. Thus, one adherent of this position, Neil McCluskey, writes: "The teaching process [in a Catholic school] may be modified by a crossplay of other legitimate aims." Quoting Robert Henle, S.J., he continues: "In the concrete, teaching activity may be carried out so as to promote virtue and to allow the influence of dedicated personalities full play." Yet McCluskey concludes: "despite their importance, however, this secondary aim must remain incidental and subordinate to the primary activity of teaching."[61]

The moderate intellectualists tend to believe that the extracurricular program of school activities exists primarily to take care of these worthwhile secondary aims. Lorenzo Reed, S.J., expresses this view succinctly when he states: "Let the school use all of its class time for the fulfillment of its primary purpose. Let it seek to achieve its secondary purposes through a carefully planned extracurricular program."[62] But as Johnston observes, "extracurricular activities are supposed to be essentially by-products of intellectual instruction, otherwise they are wasteful."[63]

It should be underscored that the intellectualists do not exclude moral-religious development from the work of the Catholic school. Rather, intellectualists see such development going on side by side with, but subordinate to, the school's primary proximate purpose, the development of the intellect. Even the strict intellectualists would gladly agree to this, though of course in a much more restricted sense than the moderate intellectualists. Thus Vincent Edward Smith, a strict intellectualist, remarks that "if everything we do, to be meritorious, must be informed by charity, the intellectual life itself can surely have such a character." Indeed, since all knowledge can contribute to the "contemplation of the highest intelligible object," it follows that "all knowledge, far from being separated from charity, can itself be meritorious." Consequently "it may be said that all institutions within the Church have for their aim to make man good; but the aim most proper to the school is to make man good intellectually."[64]

To appreciate this position properly, it is important to remember that, like Aristotle, Thomas Aquinas emphasized that man's highest faculty, and hence the mode by which he most resembles God, is man's intellect.[65] Moreover, for Aristotle and Aquinas, the highest intellectual activity is not in the practical intellect, but in the speculative intellect. The Beatific Vision is first and fundamentally an intellectual activity, an encounter of the speculative intellect of man with God.

Those parents, students, and educators who embrace a more moderate view of the intellectualist position give a greater role to the school in developing the moral and religious virtues. Thus Neil McCluskey, one of the principal spokesmen for this position, contends that the Catholic school exists primarily "to develop the morally intelligent person."[66] It should be noted here that the word "intelligent" is the substantive adjective, with the word "morally" its adverbial modifier. Therefore the primary proximate intellectualist purpose remains intact, while nevertheless indicating a substantial (but not exclusive) direction to the development of these intellectual virtues. According to advocates of this position, such as McCluskey, the moral thrust of the intellectual work of the Catholic school is deliberately effected in three separate but complementary ways: hierarchical ordering, judicious integration, and a pervasive atmosphere.

The intellectual work of the school, contend these intellectualists, should be carefully ordered to the hierarchy of values as perceived by the Catholic religion.

> The Catholic philosophy of education is based on the reality of the supernatural and its primacy in the total scheme of things. The values, goals, and ideals of the natural order—important and worthy of pursuit as these may be—are subordinate in Catholic eyes to those of the supernatural order.[67]

Thomas Donlan develops this same point when speaking of the relationship of the Catholic school within the general framework of Catholic education:

> Thus the proper and immediate end of the school is the inculcation of the intellectual virtues, but this is undertaken only in view of the proper goal of education in general, and ultimately in view of the attainment of eternal life itself.[68]

What do these key statements by McCluskey and Donlan mean in terms of specifics, such as academic subjects, extracurricular activities, guidance practices, and so forth? It is on the implementation of this point that there is a divergence of opinion on the part of those espousing the intellectualist viewpoint. One group would say with Donlan:

> If the papal demands [of Pius XI in *Divini Illius Magistri*] that error be excluded from the subjects taught and that dangerous practices be eliminated from the academic environment were to be put into the terminology of St. Thomas, it would simply be a demand that the entire school and all its parts be subjected to the sapiential judgment of theology,

which is the highest human wisdom judging all human endeavor according to the principles of faith.[69]

The school, then, is a morally responsible agency, and everything in the school must conform to the norms of morality which are known by faith and reason.[70]

Herbert Johnston develops this same point with even greater attention to specifics:

A religiously affiliated school could not be expected to condone teaching calculated to undermine the very religious beliefs and practices which it was officially encouraging. For example, a teacher who, in his course on the family, came out strongly in favor of divorce and artificial birth control could not reasonably expect to hold a position in a Catholic school. In secular schools, however, the question of academic freedom is more complicated. Finally, schools have the responsibility of so supervising their extra-class activities that no moral damage is likely to result for the students.[71]

The second group, composed of such men as Neil McCluskey, would respond somewhat differently from the Donlan-Johnston group. Thus McCluskey, while certainly upholding the ordering of the Catholic school to supernatural values, would deny that ordering either is tantamount to strict regulations or that ordering comes through the science of theology. Each specifically distinct subject area possesses its own ontological autonomy; it is not so much in the multitude of specifics but rather in the total thrust that such a hierarchical ordering unto supernatural values is legitimate or possible. Theology must be considered as a separate science, rather than as a policing discipline in the Catholic school. Theology as a science in the Catholic school must be kept distinct from faith learned through catechesis and watered by grace; it is faith more than theology which provides the germ of hierarchical ordering, especially in the moral domain. McCluskey also distinguishes between the collegiate and subcollegiate levels of Catholic schooling. At the collegiate level, the type of theological regulation of which the Donlan-Johnston group of moderate intellectualists speak is totally unwarranted, and indeed destructive of that type of theological speculation which is crucial to the development of that discipline.[72] At the subcollegiate level, however, a teacher in any subject or problem area is free to hold or discuss views such as birth control or divorce, within the norms of relevance to the course and of prudence. Only if the subcollegiate instructor's teachings or his personal life occasioned notorious public scandal of such a magnitude as to substantially hinder the work of the Catholic school in which he is engaged should he be asked to resign.[73] McCluskey adds that dismissal for notorious public scandal would not occur merely in a Catholic school but in any other kind of school as well.

Judicious integration of religious facts and values with other areas of the curriculum and school activities forms the second principal way in which the moderate intellectualists see the moral thrust of the intellectual work of the Catholic school deliberately effected. Supernatural wisdom is seen as "the supreme integrating principle" pervading the entire school.[74] Indeed, states McCluskey, even though religion or theology is taught formally as such for only a few class periods per week, its influence pervades other areas of the curriculum. However, this integration, this pervasiveness of religion into classes or activities other than religion should not be done so as to violate the autonomy of these other intellectual disciplines or activities. Rather, "religious themes receive proportionate treatment in other courses where they are integral to the subject."[75] For example, in a world history course, religious facts and themes are introduced during the treatment of the Enlightenment period in France. But this integration of religious facts and themes into class should be such as to give fullness to the subjects under discussion; they should not be done so as to render the class a disguised religion class.

A pervasive atmosphere of religion, religious values, and deep Christian living constitutes the third major way in which the moderate intellectualists see the moral thrust of the intellectual work of the school deliberately effected. In a Catholic school the child does not learn religious knowledges, however hierarchically ordered to supernatural values, or learn religious understandings however judiciously integrated into other curricular areas, in a vacuum. Rather, the entire atmosphere of the Catholic school is characterized by and promotive of a Christian sense of values, a Christian way of life. In this kind of atmosphere the religious knowledges, understandings, and values are fused into one complete whole. It is by and through this atmosphere that the student "learns that his faith is not something apart but is related to the whole texture of life."[76]

A scholion to, though in an important sense also a basis for, the intellectualist position is their contention that morality cannot be taught directly. At best, morality can be taught indirectly by the personal example of the teachers and by the impact of the Catholic atmosphere of the school. Philosophically, this contention finds its roots in the Aristotelean and Thomistic dichotomous distinction between the intellectual virtues and the moral virtues. According to Aristotle and Aquinas, the intellect is a distinct faculty which is capable of acquiring only intellectual data. The will, on the other hand, is another distinct faculty which is capable of acquiring only moral entities. Knowledge belongs to the intellect and moral action to the will. Consequently morality cannot be learned by the intellect and so is not directly teachable. Moral virtue can therefore only be fostered; it cannot be taught directly. The school's Catholic atmosphere more than anything else helps foster the acquisition of the moral virtues, contend the intellectualists.

> These [moral-religious] principles are not taught
> day by day by means of blackboard diagrams and
> class recitations. In a gentle imperceptible manner,
> however, their meaning is absorbed and they be-

come quietly operative in the life of the Catholic child. Certain traditional symbols silently telling of God, the Incarnation of His Son, man's Redemption by Christ, and the life of the blessed in heaven help to establish this atmosphere of the supernatural.[77]

Herbert Johnston nicely encapsules one wing of the intellectualist position on this question when he writes: "The teacher can do a great deal for the moral formation of his students, and he can do it best by paying no direct attention to it. Morally speaking, we teach by what we are and what we do. . . ."[78] Johnston expresses open suspicion of teachers "who were reputed to inspire their students." He questions what such teachers are inspiring students toward. He concludes by saying: "The only inspiration at which a classroom teacher should aim is inspiration to learn; the only love which he is supposed to be developing is love of learning."[79]

Some Weaknesses of the Moralist Position

Intellectualists and kindred thinkers believe that there are several serious weaknesses in the moralist position.

The first major weakness is an unrealistic conception of the school in contemporary society. By reason of the demands of a highly developed and specialized civilization, there is a heavy vocational cast to all American schools, not only at the collegiate level, but at the secondary and elementary levels as well. Schooling is more and more the best and most direct avenue to future vocational success. Even the so-called liberal arts curricula have an almost direct bearing on future career success in that these are needed for entrance into many careers and specialized schools. Indeed, the liberal arts for many Americans is itself a career, e.g., teaching and certain other social service professions. This heavy vocational bent to schooling extends down even into the elementary school, for success at this level is crucial if the student is to gain admittance to one of the many types of selective high schools or to specialized curricula in comprehensive high schools. These high schools in turn constitute indispensable rungs for entrance into the better colleges or universities. It must be noted that entrance into the selective schools at the next higher educational level does not depend on the moral-religious attainments of the student; instead, it is skill in the academic subjects, the "secular subjects," as the moralists call them, which determine entrance into the more selective upper schools. This is particularly true of entrance into Catholic secondary schools and into Catholic institutions of higher learning, most of which are rather selective in admissions. Catholic schools of today simply cannot afford to be glorified Sunday schools. Moreover, it is probably true to say that many of the unprofessional characteristics of not a few Catholic schools, e.g., overcrowded classrooms and sub-standard teaching and guidance personnel are due to a moral-ist goal of the school, as witness the spirited defense of the Curé of Ars' school by both Kevin O'Brien and Pope St. Pius X. While such unprofessional characteristics do indeed con-stitute an abuse rather than the proper use of the moralist school, nontheless there has been a strong tendency toward abuse, as history bears out. It has been partly due to the rise of an opposition to the moralist position that Catholic schools have begun to become more professionalized.

The second major weakness of the moralist position is its refusal to accord the intellectual life its due respect. Moralists tend to separate the school's program into two spheres, direct Catholic morality and the less worthy "secular" areas. This dichotomy springs from a lack of awareness of the intrinsic values of diverse realities as they are, not in the ideal order, but in the existential order. As Leo Ward, C.S.C. remarked, "In some circumstances, an inherently lower end must rate highest; for instance it is better to give a starving man some soup than to pray for him; and good as it is to pray for him, we should not let the praying get in the way of the soup."[80] Rationality is one of God's most precious gifts to man; hence it is of inestimable value, whether or not this knowledge wears the overt label "religious." The disvaluation of knowl-edge brought about by reducing it to the status of a mere means to moralist curricular ends, creates a great problem of academic freedom for Catholic schools. Indeed, such a view makes freedom to learn and the Catholic school a contradiction in terms. The papal statements cited in the previous treatment of the moralist position etch quite clearly the great threat to academic freedom posed by the moralist position. Two examples will serve to bring this out. In his *Divini Illius Magistri,* Pius XI states that only in rare instances should students in a Catholic school read authors "propounding false doctrine," and in such cases the reading must be done with a purpose of "refuting it," with "an antidote of sound doctrine."[81] But who decides whether a particular teaching constitutes false doctrine? Thus in the late 1950s and early 1960s, J. D. Salinger's novel *The Catcher in the Rye* was forbidden to be read in some Catholic secondary schools because officials there believed it was dangerous to the morals of their students. Yet in other Catholic schools the officials saw nothing wrong with this novel. Also in the same encyclical, Pius states that to be a truly Catholic school, the "whole organization of the school, its teachers, syllabus and textbooks of every kind" must be regulated according to the "Christian spirit under the direction and maternal supervision of the Church." The pontiff clearly notes that this applies to all levels of schooling, from the elementary level to the university.[82] But who is the Church? Besides, such "direction" and "supervision" clearly inhibit free inquiry and exploration which are so vital to the lifeblood of any school. As Daniel Callahan expressed it: "It is a sham to tell students they should seek the truth, but then to tell them that they are not allowed to listen to certain people's vision of the truth."[83] "Direction" and "supervision" by the Church, however maternal, sooner or later tend to degenerate into policing and constricting. In the end, to use Thomas O'Dea's words: "Correctness of formula threatens to replace understanding, while rote memorization is held to be the essence of learning."[84]

The third major weakness of the moralist position is the

lack of awareness of the value and intrinsic importance of so-called "secular" or "natural" knowledge. But as Leo Ward noted, human beings need secular knowledge.[85] Do not theologians observe that a person's degree of glory in heaven will be radically (though not exclusively) affected by the amount and degree of knowledge he possesses? God has immersed Himself in all reality. He has not confined Himself simply to that sector of reality labelled "religious." Hence, to know God adequately one must know Him as He reveals Himself in the diversity of His creation. Thus Teilhard de Chardin could movingly write: "By virtue of the Creation, and still more of the Incarnation, nothing is profane for those who know how to see."[86] To grow and develop, religion needs "secular" knowledge, not as a sycophantic handmaiden, but as a precious form of grasping reality— and therefore the God in reality—in its own autonomous right. A Christian ought to seek knowledge on its own terms rather than merely as a means to a formally labelled religious end. For, in the Teilhardian vision, knowledge is in one perspective a religious end in itself. The more a person knows, the more he can love God, since one cannot love what one does not know. The attitude of the moralists toward "secular" learning seems akin to the notion that Eve sinned because she sought more knowledge.

The fourth major weakness of the moralist position is its apparent failure to realize that the Catholic-oriented school should engage its students in a living dialogue with all reality, not just with those elements which are considered doctrinally or morally "safe" or which are regarded as directly building moral character. It was Emanuel Cardinal Suhard who noted that the education of students must "bear on pure truth and disinterested science": no apologetical interest should interfere with this free quest—rather, the student "must seek only what is."[87] To be sure, a strong current of apologeticism which has not infrequently characterized Catholic schools has led at least one intellectualist to conclude that the task of the Catholic school has often been that of "providing a life-time supply of answers to 'difficulties' to be memorized and filed away for future readiness, and often the role of the laity is conceived as having in readiness the 'Catholic answer' to give to non-Catholic friends." The same observer continues: "There seems to be an implicit notion abroad in some quarters that the Catholic mind will be the product of the catechism, the scholastic manual, and finally of the pamphlet rack."[88] Indeed, the constant concern of the moralists to protect the Catholic school student from dangers to faith or morals tends to result in a school which is more of a shelter than a school. Ghettoism is no substitute for the Christian leaven which Christ asked all his followers to become. Effective Catholic schooling constitutes a genuine risk, not a search for a rule of safety.

The fifth major weakness of the moralist position is the unwarranted creation of a great chasm between the natural and the supernatural. Kevin O'Brien nicely illustrates this dichotomy posited by the moralists: "Parents and teachers should never forget that a boy of twelve with a knowledge of the essential truths of faith is on a loftier pinnacle than a Steinmetz, an Edison, an Einstein without faith."[89] This view neglects the fact that God interpenetrates all knowledge and indeed all reality so that any divorce between natural and supernatural is more conceptual than real. The natural and the supernatural are the two sides of the one coin, but it is God who passes through the coin. Every cause is somehow and in some way in its effect; so it is with God and his creatures. Thus Walter J. Ong, S.J., could say that "God's presence in [all reality] has been undervalued, for his presence in reality is proportionate to its actuality."[90] God cannot be extricated from any reality to render it a "secular" husk. This is also true of the so-called "secular subjects" of the Catholic school curriculum. Thus Jacques Maritain remarked: "Intelligence is at the very basis of the Christian life."[91] No knowledge is secular. All knowledge is God-soaked whether that knowledge is the knowledge of an Edison or of O'Brien's hypothetical boy of twelve. The Catholic school must first and foremost be Catholic; it ought not to remand to an inferior place the development of the "natural man," because by developing the "natural man" the Catholic school is, in one very profound sense, directly developing the supernatural man. As for the student, Romano Guardini's observation is germane: the Gospel of St. John is the most human of all the gospels, which is one of the chief reasons why it is the most divine. Concerning what is studied, it is well to recall that all reality oozes God. That this is true not only of intellectual, volitional, and emotional reality, but of physical reality as well is enunciated touchingly by Teilhard who referred to concrete matter as "the great and Universal Host" which should be handled in a spirit of adoration.[92]

Some Weaknesses of the Intellectualist Position

Nor is the intellectualist position without its weaknesses, as moralists and kindred thinkers are not remiss in pointing out.

Its first major weakness is an unrealistic conception of the de facto, existential, primary proximate purpose of the Catholic school in American contemporary society. The data from the previously discussed Neuwien investigation revealed that in the opinion of the parents of Catholic school children, the overwhelming majority believe that the primary proximate purpose of the Catholic school is moral-religious. The Greeley-Rossi study of both "average" and "intellectually and liberally elite" Catholics came to precisely the same conclusion. Since the Roman Catholic Church, more than any single group in history, has asserted that it is the primary right of the parents to choose the kind of school they wish for their children, it is obvious that the primary proximate goal of the Catholic subcollegiate school is de facto moralist. Further, the Neuwien data indicate that in the perceptions of the students in Catholic elementary and secondary schools, the moral-religious goal constitutes the most important reason for their being in a Catholic school. Indeed, these students rated the intellectual-academic purpose as third, following the occupational-vocational purpose which they ranked in second place. Another way of looking at this same de facto reality is to ask oneself the question: "If in my locality the government school provided a richer intellectual diet than its Catholic school counterpart, to which school would I send my child?" It seems safe to guess that in the vast majority of cases the Catholic school would be chosen, so long as the Catholic school is not extremely deficient in intellectual training. Moreover, it seems quite clear that the episcopacy and the laity support Catholic schools, and the clergy and religious teach in them primarily for the religious formation which they believe is significantly richer there than in the local corresponding government school. If any discussion of primary proximate purposes is to bear a semblance to reality rather than to be an excursion into the rarefied atmosphere of pure speculative thought, there must of necessity be an active relationship between the real purposes and the theoretical purposes.

The second major weakness of the intellectualist position is its seeming lack of appreciation of the state of contemporary American education and schooling. By insisting on the separation of intellectual development and moral development, and by emphasizing the primacy (and in some cases the exclusivity) of the former, the intellectualists have constricted the notion of school to less than the contemporary American situation. There are many fine schools of the performing arts, schools of music, of art, and vocational schools of divers sorts—all recognized by the government and by society as legitimate secondary schools or institutions of higher learning. Schools for emotionally disturbed children constitute an integral part of several metropolitan school systems. Surely these schools do not exist primarily, much less exclusively, for intellectual development. The intellectualist concept of the school breaks down even further when the vast complex of educational television is considered. The primary proximate purpose of these TV networks, channels, and programs is intellectual; yet would such television programs constitute a school? Probably not—yet intellectualists maintain that the element which makes the school distinct from any other societal activity is that it alone exists specifically for intellectual development. In another vein, most comprehensive schools have their share of slow learners and "won't learners." By law, society compels these youths to attend school until the age of 16 or 17. Yet anyone who teaches such classes or in such schools will be quick to testify that the primary proximate goal of such classes or schools is surely not intellectual development. Today's American common schools are dedicated to serve all youth, not simply those who are primarily seeking intellectual development. And most American schools, both common schools and the upper schools, have some sort of program in pupil personnel and guidance services. Yet it is characteristic of intellectualists either to ignore the guidance function or to deny its validity. Thus Neil McCluskey in his *Catholic Viewpoint on Education* does not have a single index entry for either pupil personnel services or for guidance services; a reader of the book looks in vain for a discussion of these topics in relation to the purpose of the school. James Conant, Frank Bowles, and Frank Kerins emasculate guidance to include only scholastic guidance.[93] Vincent Edward Smith excluded all nondiscursive, noncurricular activities—hence guidance—from the true nature of the school. Yet it is interesting to note that the research has clearly shown that scholastic problems are not difficulties in themselves but are in reality functions of personality problems.[94] To be sure, every teacher, particularly at the subcollegiate level, is a guidance worker not only outside the classroom but inside it during the lesson itself.

The third major weakness of the intellectualist position is the overvaluation of knowledge. Man is composed of more than simply intellect; he has a will, emotions, a physique, all of which may play a far more important role in a person's daily decisions than does his intellect. Thus Bishop John B. McDowell observes: "The fact that while a Catholic education is in the business of giving knowledge and understanding about life as we Catholics accept it, this is simply not enough. There are habits and skills of living that are *equally* important . . . Knowledge is important, but it is not enough."[95] Indeed, knowledge and virtue are not identical. Yet despite their assertions to the contrary, the intellectualists seem unavoidably to imply that once knowledge—even McCluskey's moral intelligence—is learned in the school, the students will thereby be led to pursue "the good life." It might be said that a natural practical conclusion of this view was developed by a sister-teacher in a Catholic secondary school who believed that a person who performed a deed which he knew was wrong was a "weakling" or simply "lacked respect for authority."[96] The Catholic school is fundamentally incomplete if it only teaches about virtue; it should afford the students an opportunity to practice it. Indeed, with their heavy emphasis on knowledge and the intellectual life, intellectualists typically do not stress the cruciality of what John Childs terms "primary experience" in classroom activities.[97] But it is precisely this secondhandedness of experience which accounts for the mediocrity of much of schooling. Learning about something can never substitute for learning something.

The fourth major weakness of the intellectualist position is that all learning, even all conceptual learning, is not directly intellectual. The findings of psychologists have shown that a great deal of learning, and indeed often the most influential and most meaningful kind, is acquired by other than purely intellectual means. A person gains concepts not simply by means of his intellect, but through emotional experiences, physical encounters, love, and so forth. The texture of each of these modes of conceptual knowing is rich and varied, and contributes to the fullness of knowledge. One might intellectually speculate about the essence of a pirouette, but the ballerina who is actually performing the pirouette has a much different, probably a much more accurate, and surely a much richer concept of a pirouette. The notion that the intellect can know only through the mental was one of the doctrines of the old Wolffian faculty psychology, a doctrine which can be seriously questioned (and indeed fundamentally challenged) in view of the findings of modern behavioral science. Correlative to the point developed in this paragraph, intellectualists seem to imply that knowledge can be imparted. This is particularly true of Smith with his emphasis on teaching as a strictly discursible form. Yet knowledge in different persons is analogical and not univocal. Consequently, it is psychologically impossible to transmit knowledge from teacher to student. There is no transfusion of learning in the sense that there is a transfusion of blood. Emphasis on the analogical structure of learning, with stress on carefully structured personal experience by the student, constitutes the most effective approach to teaching. If intellectualists such as Johnston and Smith believe that morality cannot be taught directly, it is precisely because they limit direct teaching to intellectual means, particularly to the discursive. Since morality is nonintellectual, it is obvious that these intellectualists are begging the question. If teaching is brought out from the oxcart stage wherein it is considered strictly an intellectual activity and placed in the contemporary context wherein it is defined as "structuring the situation whereby learning is caused," then it is clear that almost anything, morality included, can be taught. This conclusion opens an entirely new avenue for consideration of the primary proximate purpose of the Catholic school.

The fifth major weakness of the intellectualist position is its vagueness and amorphousness. Several of the intellectualists speak rather fondly about some sort of "Catholic atmosphere" which is supposed to suffuse the entire school program. But what precisely is this "Catholic atmosphere"? How does one know it is there? Does it have any degrees, so that a school can improve its atmosphere level? It is so easy for a religious institute or for a Catholic parent to claim a particular school has a Catholic atmosphere; but how does one know with any measure of certitude whether or not this "atmosphere" is in reality a wishful projection? An agent of society, such as the school, which is supposed to exemplify a conscious, deliberate, carefully structured program for learning, can hardly take refuge in the opaque mists of "atmosphere." Yet another zone in which several of the intellectualists exhibit amorphousness is in their contention that it is theology which provides the supreme integrating factor in the Catholic school. Such a notion presents several difficulties, not the least of which is the impossibility for any one single branch of knowledge to serve as the integrating principle for all the others. To be an integrating force, an entity cannot be a particular (such as theology or history) but rather a universal. To be integrational, a reality must contain within itself those elements common to each individual reality to be integrated. Surely theology, which is a distinct mode of intellectual inquiry set aside fundamentally from other modes of inquiry, cannot hope to integrate biology or geography or mathematics. In the practical order, concrete integration of the Catholic school curriculum has rarely been attempted.[98] Actually, it was the intellectualists more than any other group who both conceptually and in practice indicated their opposition to the Core curriculum, one of the few empirically verified attempts at achieving genuine curricular integration.[99] Finally, into the question of "hierarchical ordering" of the school of which the intellectualists speak, the thorny problem of academic freedom intrudes itself. As was seen before, the positions of Donlan and Johnston on the supreme role of theology (and Christian mores) as the hierarchical orderer(s) of the Catholic school basically curtails academic freedom. However, other intellectualists like McCluskey staunchly uphold academic freedom on all levels of Catholic schooling. John Walsh, C.S.C., expressed this second wing of intellectualism thus:

> The Catholic university, i.e., the community of scholars and learners at a Catholic university, recognizes the autonomy of the various disciplines and of the various professors and students working within these disciplines. Each discipline discovers or creates its own truth and its own value. Theology

> could not, even if it should so desire, dictate the
> content or direction of learning in the other dis-
> ciplines. Rather theology learns from the other dis-
> ciplines, just as they learn from it.[100]

Walsh's carefully-stated position shows that the entire principle of the hierarchical ordering by any single intellectual
discipline is out of joint with a Catholic university. (Indeed, it probably is true though in lesser degrees for the
Catholic elementary and Catholic secondary schools). Walsh's
statement indicates how the entire concept of curricular
integration is fundamentally at sharp variance with the
intellectualist position. To be sure, American Catholic universities, which by and large are controlled by the intellectualists, are increasingly becoming secular in orientation.
Whether this is being done in an effort to achieve academic
excellence, or to help solve financial problems, or from other
motives is uncertain. Yet Philip Gleason's remark in this
connection is quite cogent:

> In what sense is a Catholic university Catholic if it
> is composed predominantly of lay professors who
> employ, in their teaching and research, the same
> methods and norms as their counterparts in secular
> universities, and who are engaged in the pursuit of
> knowledge in autonomous spheres that are in no
> way dependent upon any over-all "Catholic posi-
> tion?"[101]

And what about non-Catholic professors in Catholic universities, professors who neither know nor are vitally concerned
with Catholicism or with Catholic thought? In such cases—
and they are multiplying—where is the hierarchical ordering,
where is the judicious integration, where is the pervasive
Catholic atmosphere? The same is true for Catholic secondary
schools whose teaching ranks are being more and more filled
by non-Catholic teachers. Where is the hierarchical ordering
or judicious integration in the Catholic dental school? And
where is the Catholic atmosphere in a certain metropolitan
eastern Catholic university whose dean of the college of edu-

cation told the present writer that Catholic textbooks could not be used there for fear of "offending the students," nearly 90 percent of whom were non-Catholic?

The Integralist Position

The foregoing analyses would seem to indicate that neither the moralist nor the intellectualist position provides a complete and adequate answer to the primary proximate purpose of the Catholic school. What is needed, then, is a new approach to the primary proximate purpose of Catholic schooling. This new approach can come about, not by a total rejection of the moralist and intellectualist positions, but rather from sublimating the best elements of these positions and adding to them some essentially different and fresh ingredients.

The primary proximate purpose of the Catholic school should be a fusion of understanding, action, and love *co-equally*. By "co-equally" here is meant that the development of each of these educational outcomes is sought by the Catholic school co-extensively with the others. None of the three, consequently, is supreme, causing the other two to be ordered unto it. The sweet combination of the three in one bundle constitutes the purpose of Catholic schooling. It is this bundle of three co-equal components, none of which is complete without the other two, to which the name "integralist" is given by the present writer.

To grasp the integralist position adequately, it is necessary to have a clear notion of each of its three constituents. Understanding is here defined as the deepest, most penetrating, and most meaningful grasp and appreciation of reality.[102] Understanding plumbs all of reality, from the surface to its very depths. Further, and axially, understanding seizes reality from the vantage point of that very reality itself, rather than from the standpoint of the person experiencing that reality. Understanding comes only from the total grasp of reality, a grasp composed of intellectual, emotional, and physical apprehension. Consequently, understanding cannot be attained by study or by any other vicarious means; rather, understanding can only be gained from knowledge plus experience. Thus it is possible for a person to be intelligent and even wise, but to lack understanding. Conversely, understanding necessitates both knowledge and wisdom, to which are added experience and the apprehension of the reality from its own existential standpoint.

Action is here defined as a performance. Now this performance need not be in the concrete order, such as the giving of alms to a missioner. Action can also be done in the quiet of one's own being. But in all cases, action consists of the internal or external carrying through of some thought, some desire, or some emotion. To this extent action objectifies understanding (which of its nature is wholly subjective).

Love is here defined as the going out of oneself and becoming one with some segment of reality, not primarily for one's own sake but rather principally for the sake of that reality. Love, then, is the going out to a slice of reality rather than the grasping and the bringing in of some reality. (The grasping and the bringing in are fruits of love, rather than its essence.) Love is the raising up to the level of relational intersubjectivity two otherwise unrelated slices of reality. Love represents this fusion because in love understanding and action melt into one. Understanding is a vital constituent of love because without understanding love would fade into the realm of subhuman desire or brutish appetency. Action is an essential ingredient of love because without action love would be reduced to the category of an unfulfilled wish. However, when love is spoken of as a synthesis of understanding and action, this does not mean a combination of action and love alone, for there is in love a third ingredient, much more elusive and harder to pinpoint. This third element, the dynamic sublational impulsion, is that inexplicable attraction which one reality has for the other which draws one irresistibly toward the other, and in the case of reciprocated human love, which draws them to each other. It is love, that highest synthesis of the finest elements of reality, which

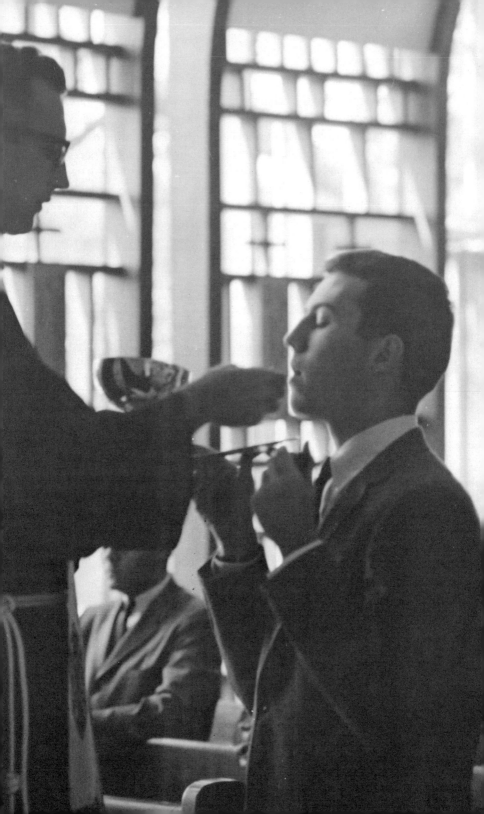

represents the supreme value, particularly in the post-Redemptive world.

Understanding, action, and love—the three essential, co-equal components of the integralist position—should not be conceived as tight, unrelated entities. They are not dichotomous or mutually exclusive like the intellectual virtues and the moral virtues of Aristotle and the Scholastics. Rather, each flows into the others, enriching the others and in turn being enriched by the others. Thus, for example, understanding fructifies action, while action, as Dewey so clearly explained it, tends to beget and to deepen understanding. Understanding presupposes possession of the truth; yet as St. Paul stressed, not only is the truth itself important, but "doing the truth" is also essential. The insights of the "new theology" and of modern philosophers such as Gabriel Marcel have indicated that truth is not a mere sterile intellectual datum, but a living reality. For the Christian, truth is fundamentally a Person, Jesus. Thus when asked by Pilate "What is truth?", Jesus did not reply verbally because an intellectual datum would not be the accurate answer. Instead, Jesus responded to Pilate with His Presence, for there, in the Person, resided the true and total answer. Hence, understanding is incomplete without action, and vice versa. And since it was by love more than by anything else that Jesus showed the world He was divine, it is into love that understanding and action must be synthesized if these two are to fulfill themselves. In terms of specifics in the context of the school's primary proximate purpose, it is clear that understanding a foreign language is not sufficient; the student must also have proficiency (action) in it. To illustrate this point further: the moralist position would be fulfilled if a student in religion class at Saint Cuthbert's Academy practiced the precepts of his religion, even though he did not know the basic reasons behind these precepts. Of course the moralist would be pleased if the student also knew the foundations for the precepts but the knowledge is not essential; at best, it is a means to the end. The intellectualist position would be fulfilled if the boy grasped clearly the teachings of the Faith, even though outside of class or school he did not practice them. Such a student could therefore receive an "A" in religion class, yet be a poor Catholic outside of class or school. Of course the intellectualist would be pleased if the student acted on his knowledge, but this action is not essential to the primary proximate purpose of the class or the school. The integralist position could not be fulfilled unless the student understood, acted, and loved his religion as learned in the religion class (and in the rest of the school as well).

Thus it is essential to the integralist position that the Catholic school represent a careful pedagogical structuring so as to effect personality transformation. The school is not merely an institution which somehow juridically stands "in loco parentis." It is a society in which the student grows, and through which he forges his personality. The integralist-oriented school will so integrate understanding, action, and love into the learning texture that the student, who by virtue of being in the school is existentially a part of that texture, is profoundly transformed as well. As Allen Wheelis [103] and Erik Erikson [104] have observed, the school is one of the most crucial milieux for exploring, shaping, and forging one's own identity. Since the Christian student's identity lies in Jesus, in understanding Him, in acting upon Him, and in loving Him, it is obvious that these three virtues must characterize the Catholic school's essence.

The foregoing analysis, particularly the above paragraph, clearly indicates that to be meaningful, realistic, and effective, the primary proximate purpose of the school must be radicated in each student himself. From the psychological point of view, this is an absolute necessity inasmuch as the primary proximate cause of learning is the student himself. It is only to the extent that the student makes the purposes of the school his very own that the purposes of the school, however praiseworthy, become real and living. In a conflict between the student's purposes and the school's purposes, the school rarely if ever wins. From another angle, it ought to be remembered that in a very real sense the student forms an essential and indispensable part of the school. Therefore, to the extent that the school's goals are not the student's goals is the school less of a school. The Catholic school must not only structure the learning situation so that the student acquires values, but to a great extent to structure the situation so that the student is led to create his own values. This does not mean to imply that the student should be encouraged to structure his own values without any regard to Christ and the Church; rather, it means that in structuring his own values, he should incorporate the Christian values into a viable, vibrant, and personal guide for fruitful living.

"The educational process," wrote John Dewey, "is one of continued reorganizing, reconstructing, transforming."[105] It is within the school that the student ought to have the freedom to live and to externalize his own purposes. Now this does not suggest a totally permissive, laissez-faire school. Rather, it means that the instructional and guidance staffs of the Catholic school work closely with the students to develop together the specific concretizations of the integralist triad of understanding, action, and love. In the absence of such deep student involvement, the purposes of the school, thrust on the unwitting youths from outside and above, will at best be cooperated with for the sake of gamesmanship or fear of failing, or at worst will be rejected outright by the students. The school is a preparation for Christian living only to the extent that it is the fullness of present Christian living for that stage of the student's development. Only present living can prepare a person for future living.

The Catholic school at every level, then, is a deliberate, conscious apostolate of the Church. It is this which makes the school purposive as an agency of the institutional Church. This was made abundantly and repeatedly clear in Vatican II's *Declaration on Christian Education*. Because of its apostolic thrust, the primary proximate goal of the Catholic school must include in its very fiber the Christian reconstruction of the individual as well as of society. It would seem that in contrast to purposes which are less integrational, less structured, and less complete, the integralist position provides for the conscious and deliberate realization of this apostolically reconstructional thrust. Eschewed by the integralist position is the restrictive Newmanistic Irish mountain-top view of the Catholic school's purpose. To Herbert Johnston's statement that "knowledge, as Newman put it for all time, is its own end, worth having for what it is",[106] the integralist would answer with John McDowell: "Knowledge is important, but it is not enough," and "whether it likes it or not, the school is not developing intellect—it is developing personalities."[107] Christian reconstruction of the student constitutes a fundamental reorientation, and it is through the triad of understanding, action, and love that this reconstruction can most efficaciously take place. Naturally, each school level from kindergarten through the university will tailor the integralist triad to its own exigencies and concrete existential situation. Nonetheless the triad remains. And the presence of each element of this triad assures that the apostolic thrust of the Catholic school does not degenerate into a pietistic approach.

Integration has always been one of the most hoped-for outcomes of the Catholic school. Yet as was indicated earlier in this book, no one academic subject, whether it be theology or any other discipline, nor any one wisdom, be it supernatural wisdom or any other, can provide integration. Integration cannot result from any one particular; only a universal in which many particulars participate (to use Plato's fruitful notion) can provide integration. But for a Catholic school, integration ought not to remain solely in the intellectual order; nor ought it to remain solely in the unified confederation of many intellectual disciplines made one by any integrational principle. Rather, in a Catholic school —this exquisite vehicle for the apostolate—integration must be both horizontal and vertical. It must be horizontal in the sense that it integrates the intellectual areas studied in the school. It ought to be vertical in that it unites the intellectual with real-life activities. Integralistically speaking, the Catholic school ought to integrate understanding, action, and love into a single bundle.

Christian living is the only entity powerful enough and all-encompassing enough to provide this horizontal and vertical integration. To be effective as well as real, this integration must take place in the being, in the actuality of the learner. Further, it can only be the learner, not some outside agency, who can dynamically effect this integration. To be sure, it is the key purpose and role of the school to structure the possibility and indeed the means whereby understanding, action, and love are integrated by the student. After all, if the integrational process were left totally up to the students, if the teachers and the program of themselves did not provide the structure whereby integration could be achieved by the students, then truly the students ought to be the teachers and the teachers ought to be the students.

To fulfill this integrational aim, the school program must essentially be a structured social laboratory in Christian living. It must be structured because only if the program is conscious and deliberative can there be a reasonable hope of integration. Vague hopes for a Christian educational "atmosphere" are not compatible with a planned series of experiences from which there is justified expectancy for fruitful outcomes. The school must be social because it is a gathering of human beings engaged in the joint activity of growth through interpersonal endeavor. The school is not a multiplication of individualistic tutorial sessions. Finally, the Christian school must be a laboratory, a place of developmental interaction in which students, placed in a learning environment structured to promote growth, will fulfill in themselves the purposes of the school.

To exhibit all of the above properties, the school ought to be basically a little Christian community, or perhaps more properly speaking, little Christian communities. In such a deeply personalized milieu, in which the natural and the supernatural flow through each other, the fusion of understanding, action, and love can take place in the integrational context of Christian living. In such a Christian community, the entire question of the "hierarchical ordering" of learning experiences finds a natural rather than a forced solution. By placing hierarchical ordering in the context of Christian living, the barrier between ordering to subjective hierarchies and ordering to objective hierarchies crumbles. There are times when subjective considerations take precedence over experiences which objectively speaking might be considered higher. This is nicely brought out by the illustration given by Leo Ward and cited earlier in this book whereby feeding a starving native exercises a greater hierarchy than teaching him the truths of Catholicism, even though in the "objective" sphere the latter might hold a higher hierarchical place. It is Christian living in all its actuality and richness which places learning experiences in their proper hierarchy, with the touchstone being the notion that hierarchy of learning experiences is determined by what most fruitfully advances the most efficacious Christian living in terms of the integralist triad.

The stance of Vatican II's *Declaration on Christian Education* concerning the primary proximate goal of the school is not altogether clear. There are two passages in the document, numbers five and eight respectively, which appear at variance with one another. Section five seems to take a modified intellectualist position:

> Among all the agencies of education the school has a special importance. By virtue of its very purpose, while it cultivates the intellect with unremitting attention, the school ripens the capacity for right judgment, provides an introduction into the cultural heritage won by past generations, promotes a sense of values, and readies for professional life. By creating friendly contacts between students of diverse temperament and background, the school fosters among them a willingness to understand one another. Moreover, the school sets up a kind of center whose operation and progress deserve to engage the

joint participation of families, teachers, various kinds of cultural, civic, and religious groups, civil society, and the entire human community.[108]

An analysis of the context of this text, and indeed of the passage itself, would seem to indicate that the council Fathers were here talking about a school in general rather than about a Catholic school in particular. It is section eight in which the *Declaration* specifically treats of the distinctive purposes of Catholic schools:

The Church's involvement in the field of education is demonstrated especially by the Catholic school. No less than other schools does the Catholic school pursue cultural goals and the natural development of youth. But it has several distinctive purposes. It aims to create for the school community an atmosphere enlivened by the gospel spirit of freedom and charity. It aims to help the adolescent in such a way that the development of his own personality will be matched by the growth of that new creation which he became by baptism. It strives to relate all human culture eventually to the news of salvation, so that the light of faith will illumine the knowledge which students gradually gain of the world, of life, and of mankind.

So it is that while the Catholic school fittingly adjusts itself to the circumstances of advancing times, it is educating its students to promote effectively the welfare of the earthly city, and preparing them to serve the advancement of the reign of God. The purpose in view is that by living an exemplary and apostolic life, the Catholic graduate can become, as it were, the saving leaven of the human family.[109]

This passage from the *Declaration* which deals directly with the purposes of the Catholic schools seems much broader than the intellectualist or moralist positions. It would appear to incorporate the understanding, action, and love triad of the integralist position. Yet in all candor, it cannot be said with any conclusive measure of certainty that the *Declaration* endorses the integralist position, since the pertinent texts are not clear on the point, and indeed do not always seem to manifest the highest level of internal consistency. The best which can be said is that the *Declaration's* treatment of the purposes of the Catholic school, in both the textual and contextual view, seem closer to the integralist position than to either the intellectualist or moralist view.

In a textual analysis of the *Declaration* so as to divine its nuances and basic thrust on specific points such as the primary proximate purpose, it is well to situate the *Declaration* itself into the moment in conciliar history in which it was born. To be sure, its history was a stormy one. The original schema, in the highest category of conciliar importance, was entitled *Constitution on Catholic Schools,* and was drawn up by a commission which was charged to consider seminary studies, university work, and Catholic schools. The first two texts of the constitution, viz., the 1962 and 1963 texts, were roundly criticized by many, including the United States hierarchy. By late 1963 it was apparent that the council was beginning to run out of time on all its business; deletions and shortcuts of schemata of lesser priority were necessary. It was then that the schema on Christian schools was reduced from a constitution to a *votum,* the lowest category of a conciliar document. However, several key people were able to exert sufficient influence to bring the original schema out from limbo. It was then modified, revised from a consideration of schools to the broader notion of education, raised in status, and finally debated on the floor of St. Peter's from November 17-19, 1964.[110] But even here, the future Declaration was beset with difficulties. Only a short three-day debate in St. Peter's was permitted. Yet even more importantly, the deepest concern of the council Fathers at the time of its debate centered around the so-called November crisis concerning the famous Schema 13, *The Church in the Modern World,* and also the schema dealing with religious liberty. Consequently the Fathers understandably probably gave somewhat less than full concern and attention to the schema on education. To such an extent was this the case that Paul-Émile Cardinal Leger of Montreal made an intervention[111] during the debate in St. Peter's to the effect that the council had neither the time nor the strength for an adequate examination of the schema on Christian education.[112] Indeed, the council Fathers were so tired that "perhaps they lacked the necessary physical energy to give proper care to an examination of the schema."[113] Thus, said the Cardinal, "we should not approve too hastily what will be the *Magna Carta* of Christian education."[114] Archbishop George Beck of Liverpool remarked that the document on Christian education was short, uneven, and constituted a vague, general statement.[115] After these and other interventions, including some important American ones, the document, now somewhat modified but not so substantially as to reduce the fundamental validity of the Leger-Beck objections, was favorably voted on by the council Fathers on October 13, 1965, and officially proclaimed by Paul VI fifteen days later. A post-conciliar commission is expected to develop the council's position at greater length. Until this commission's report is eventually released, there doubtless will remain some ambiguity as to the precise, unequivocal position of Vatican II and its official spirit relating to the primary proximate purpose of the Catholic school.

Not so equivocal and open to speculation is the position of the National Catholic Educational Association (NCEA). This association has never published one set of primary proximate purposes which it intended for all types and levels of American Catholic schools. Nonetheless in 1944, after long, careful, and comprehensive deliberation, the Policies Committee of the Secondary School Department of NCEA did publish an official statement entitled "Objectives of the Catholic High School."[116]

Strictly speaking, the NCEA official statement applies only to Catholic secondary schools. However, the breadth of the statement would seem to indicate that these goals or purposes can apply with equal cogency to Catholic elementary schools as well as to Catholic institutions of higher learning. Indeed, the goals are so stated that they readily admit of easy application to any school level.

The formulators of the NCEA official statement deliberately attempted to express the objectives in meaningful concrete language, in terms of behavior. Thus, instead of expressing its major objectives in such abstract terms as intelligence, morality, culture, health, and so forth, it states the goals in dynamic terms.[117]

The NCEA official statement lists seven primary proximate goals. These objectives, whose overall result is intended to "guide, nourish and stimulate the adolescent mind and heart,"[118] are: to develop intelligent Catholics, to develop spiritually vigorous Catholics, to develop cultured Catholics, to develop healthy Catholics, to develop vocationally-prepared Catholics, to develop social-minded Catholics, and to develop American Catholics.

If one were to boil down these seven primary proximate goals into basic categories, the result would be quite similar to the integralist triad of understanding, action, and love. Surely the NCEA goals are much broader and richer than are the goals of either the moralists or the intellectualists. This can be appreciated not only by examining the seven NCEA primary proximate goals themselves, but also by analyzing the components of each of these goals as elaborated by the NCEA statement. By reason of limitation of space, all the components of each of the seven goals cannot be listed; however, representative ones will be cited to show the expansive flavor of the NCEA goals—a flavor which brings the NCEA statement and the integralist position into congruance.

Under its first category of developing intelligent Catholics, the NCEA statement emphasizes the acquisition of the common store of secular knowledge, a reasonably thorough understanding of Catholic practice, and an interest in intellectual creation as well as in assimilation. In its second category, developing spiritually vigorous Catholics, the NCEA statement stresses the personalization of truth—especially moral and religious truth—by the application of it in conduct, by the habitual acting on Christian principle with an emphasis on using reason and Faith as direct instruments of self-fulfillment, and by the exercising of dynamic leadership in the lay apostolate. In its third category, developing cultured Catholics, the NCEA statement underscores the recognition of beauty in all reality whether or not overtly religious, the support of and participation in art and music and drama, and the cultivation of the proper use of imagination. In its fourth category, developing healthy Catholics, the NCEA statement points up the wise use of the body through exercise and physical self-control.

In its fifth category, developing vocationally-prepared Catholics, the NCEA statement emphasizes the mastering of knowledge and skills which will be useful in post-school life, the importance of thought and guidance in preparing for future lifework, and the development of the person to step into a meaningful occupation or into further training immediately upon leaving school. In its sixth category, developing social-minded Catholics, the NCEA statement stresses the development of a genuine love of family life, and the cultivation of essential family virtues. In its seventh category, developing American Catholics, the NCEA statement emphasizes the building up of loyalty to country, the behaving as loyal upright citizens, and the preparation to fulfill their duties as full-fledged citizens.

What is of relevance in the NCEA statement is that these are the goals which the Catholic school is supposed to produce. Hence the Catholic school's purpose is seen more broadly and more expansively than that of intellectual development or moral formation.

Critics of the integralist position on the primary proximate purpose of the Catholic school might raise the following objection: "How is the school essentially different from the other agencies of education? Do not the parish church and the hospital, for example, attempt to develop within the child

understanding, knowledge, and love? What, then, is it that makes the school fundamentally distinct?" The answer to this objection is twofold. First, the triad of co-equal purposes of the integralist position is so fundamentally distinct from the specific purpose of other agencies in range of inclusiveness as to render the Catholic school fundamentally (but not totally) distinct from the parish church or the hospital. (After all, even the moralist and the intellectualist purposes are not totally distinct from the purposes of the parish church or the hospital.) The parish church in its liturgical and paraliturgical services does indeed attempt to develop the integralist triad. However, its primary thrust is limited to providing that living sacramental relationship between God and His creature whereby that creature pays direct homage to God, and where in turn, at God's pleasure, the creature can receive from God through the liturgy and paraliturgy some measure of understanding, action, and love. However, this reception, whether as a part of the liturgical celebration or as an outcome of it, is usually restricted to the specifically labelled religious dimension. If, for example, a Church service evolves into one long meeting devoted to a consideration of civil rights activities, then the service is, properly speaking, no longer a liturgical service or a Church function, but rather a social work activity sponsored by the Church. In the instance of the hospital, it also attempts to develop the integralist triad in the child but in a radically different range and for a fundamentally different purpose than is the case in the school.

The second major factor which from the integralist position makes the Catholic school a distinctive agency of Catholic education is the fact that the school is a purposive, deliberative organization which exists to consciously shape growth by providing structured learning experiences. This is a vastly different thing from an educational agency which is characterized by some sort of vague, amorphous, and highly tenuous "Catholic atmosphere." These experiences which the school carefully structures are provided with a conscious effort to cause the student to learn, i.e., to effect a change in his behavior. This change in behavior is not only in physical behavior such as occurs in a hospital, or in religious behavior such as occurs in a parish church. Rather, this learned behavior is a result of a careful, conscious, and structured fusion of understanding (including the knowledges which help comprise understanding), action, and love. It is for this reason that in modern times the school occupies such a privileged place in each American community, for the school is the only agency of education where such a conscious and complete integration is dynamically structured and effected.

Some moralists might accuse the integralists of going counter to Pius XI's *Divini Illius Magistri* which vigorously upheld the moralist position. The answer to this objection is twofold. First, Vatican II's *Declaration on Christian Education* in one very large sense can be said to represent an advance in the magisterium's thinking. And, as was previously shown, the *Declaration* itself is not without a certain ambiguousness concerning the primary proximate purpose of the Catholic school. To be sure, one valid interpretation of the document is that it incorporates the integralist position. The second answer to the moralist objection consists in the distinction between infallible and noninfallible statements of the popes. Actually, no one has ever asserted that the primary purpose of the Catholic school as enunciated by Pius XI constitutes an infallible papal statement. Of course, encyclical pronouncements are not to be taken lightly, nor disagreed with rashly. One might argue, for example, that to the papal mind of 1929, only the intellectualist and moralist positions were available, and the pontiff chose the moralist over the intellectualist. A third and new position had not then been proposed; hence the encyclical, with its choice of only one of two positions, might fruitfully be rethought in the light of a third position, of the new findings of the behavioral sciences, and of the statements of Vatican II's *Declaration on Christian Education.*

Finally, one may ask which of the three positions on the primary proximate purpose is most easily applied to *all*

Catholic schools? Which position is most at home with schools at all levels, from kindergarten to graduate school? Which position is most comfortable in the myriad types of schools, ranging from college-prep schools to trade schools to schools engaged in special education? And which position is most compatible with Catholic schools in highly developed localities, in semi-developed areas, and in the so-called "emerging" regions? On the last mentioned area, Bishop Simon Hoa Nguyen-van-Hien of Dalat, Vietnam, observed, in the St. Peter's debate on the schema on Christian education at Vatican II, that any statement on Catholic schools should be distinctive enough to function as a *raison d'être* for the Catholic school as a separate agency, yet broad enough to cover all Catholic schools including those in the mission lands.[119] The answer to the questions posed in this paragraph surely is the integralist position.

Some Secondary Proximate Purposes

The existence of a primary proximate purpose of Catholic schooling does not automatically exclude the presence of secondary proximate purposes. In fact, every organization has a network of secondary aims. The important thing is that these secondary aims ought not to usurp the primary proximate purpose. Sometimes financial pressures, sometimes local exigencies, sometimes vocation shortages, and other times unexplained pragmatism turn a school topsy-turvy in terms of its purposes, so that the secondary purposes become the guiding principles of the school.

Other legitimate secondary proximate purposes of Catholic schools are: to serve as a means of attracting students to the clerical or religious life; to fulfill the educational apostolate of the religious institute operating the school; to serve as a Christian witness-institution in the community; and to provide a special institution for the socially or economically elite of the community.

Conclusion

This book is not intended as a pleasant academic exercise

or a sterile theoretical treatise. Its purpose is to codify and clarify existing thought on the primary proximate purpose of Catholic schooling so that parents, students, and Catholic school staffs can be in a better position to consciously structure their school program in such a way as to secure the optimal realization of this purpose. In a very crucial way the primary proximate purpose of the school is a vital force in determining the instructional strategies, the guidance modalities, and the program thrust of the entire Catholic school.

First and foremost, the Catholic school belongs to the parents. It is they who financially support the school. It is their children who attend the school. And as both the United States Supreme Court (Oregon decision) and the Roman Catholic Church have insisted, the parents do have the primary right in education. But the school also belongs to the students. It is their lives which are being affected. It is they who in the final analysis determine the school's primary proximate purpose by their own personal decisions on what that purpose is, regardless of what the "outside" and external school policy says it is. The school also belongs to the Church which includes all the community's People of God, from bishop to nonparents to the staff of the Catholic school itself. Therefore, in order to evolve the purpose of a particular Catholic school, together with the modes of its implementation, it is incumbent upon every Catholic school community— parents, students, and People of God—to work together as a cooperative group to hammer out this purpose. The Catholic school is not a "pedagarchy," a benevolent dictatorship of educators deciding the purposes and operation of the Catholic school. The Catholic school should be catholic not only in outlook but in the universality of persons deciding its purposes. Only then will it have taken the first step toward being truly Catholic.

Effective Catholic schooling for the decisive decades ahead demands a clear concept of the distinctive purpose of the Catholic school qua Catholic and qua school. Msgr. James Donohue, Director of the Department of Education, United

States Catholic Conference, expresses this axial point when he said: "And I greatly fear unless we soon offer the world a convincing *raison d'être* for Christian education, unless we soon outline in bold strokes a vision for Catholic schools that speaks to the heart of the human condition as we find it today, we will have failed."[120] Today's Church, and tomorrow's Church, cannot afford to have its schools become a fossil in the living waters, a pillar of irrelevancy in a world of intense meaningfulness. If each and every Catholic school is to fulfill its vital and distinctive purpose, then it must first have a clear concept of precisely what is its purpose. This is not at all to imply that the rest of the school program will take care of itself. But at least the rest of the program can have the supreme advantage of being built on a solid foundation.

NOTES

1. Arthur Clutton-Brock, quoted in Jacques Maritain, *Education at the Crossroads*. New Haven, Conn.: Yale University Press, 1943, pp. 23-24.

2. The Second Vatican Council in its *Declaration on Christian Education* did provide certain guidelines as to the specific purpose of the Catholic school. This will be discussed later on in this book.

3. Neil G. McCluskey, for example, expressed this view at the Eduposium sponsored by the Dominican Sisters of Racine, Wisconsin, in April, 1967. C. Albert Koob, O.Praem., Executive Secretary of the National Catholic Educational Association who shared the panel with McCluskey, did not disagree with McCluskey's view.

4. Neil G. McCluskey elaborated on this thesis in several conversations with the present writer during the spring and summer of 1967. The notions of Christian witnessing in the temporal order and the necessity of nonghettoistic catholicity in a person's schooling constitute two of the more important foundations upon which McCluskey builds and develops his thesis.

5. Andrew M. Greeley and Peter H. Rossi, *The Education of Catholic Americans*. Chicago: Aldine, 1966. Michael Schiltz, senior study director of NORC (which sponsored the investigation) discussed this finding at length in conversation with the present writer.

6. 26 U.S. 510, 45 Sup. Ct. 571.

7. Edward L. Heston, C.S.C., "Session No. 3, News Bulletin No. 43, General Congregation, No. 122," *Concilio Ecumenico Vaticano II*. Rome: Ufficio Stampa, privately duplicated and circulated, November 14, 1964, p. 4.

8. Second Vatican Council, *Declaration on Christian Education*, in Walter M. Abbott, S.J., general editor, *The Documents of Vatican II*, translated under the direction of Msgr. Joseph Gallagher. New York: Herder and Herder, and Association Press, 1966, p. 642.

9. For Thomas Bouquillon's views, see his pamphlet, *Education: To Whom Does It Belong?* Baltimore: Murphy, 1891.

10. *Declaration loc. cit.*

11. Historically, of course, the reverse was true in the United States. Church-related schools were typically founded first; the government later erected its own schools as a protest against the religious orientation of the private schools.

12. Papal statements such as *Quadragesimo Anno* and *Mater et Magistra* have utilized the principle of subsidiarity, though usually in a socioeconomic context. See Pius XI, *Quadragesimo Anno*, in *Acta Apostolicae Sedis*, XXIII (June 1, 1931), p. 203; John XXIII, *Mater et Magistra*, in *Acta Apostolicae Sedis*, LIII (July 15, 1961), p. 414.

13. Thomas Aquinas, *Summa Theologica*, I-II, q.1, a.1, ad 1. Free translation by the present writer.

14. See Henri Grenier, *Thomistic Philosophy: Moral Philosophy*, vol. IV, translated by J. P. E. O'Hanley. Charlottetown, Canada: St. Dunstan's University, 1950, p. 25.

15. Aquinas, *op. cit.*, II-II, q.23, a.8.

16. John Dewey, *Experience and Nature*. Chicago: Open Court, 1925. pp. 109-110.

17. Most Rev. Ernest J. Primeau, "Foreword," in Mary Perkins Ryan, *Are Parochial Schools the Answer?* New York: Holt, Rinehart, and Winston, 1964, p. v. Bishop Primeau defined this in the text as the purpose of Catholic education; however, the context of his remark, and indeed his whole Foreword, indicate that he is referring to the Catholic educational system, i.e., the Catholic school.

18. This inscription was so meaningful to Jung that he placed it above the doorway of his villa.

19. Neil G. McCluskey, *Catholic Viewpoint in Education*, 2d ed. Garden City, N. Y.: Doubleday, 1962, p. 58.

20. Aquinas, *op cit.*, I, q.1, a.8, ad 2.

21. The term "probably" is used advisedly here, because the present writer is unaware of any hard data on the subject; however, soft data seem to confirm this view.

22. Kevin O'Brien, C.S.S.R., *The Proximate Aim of Education*. Milwaukee: Bruce, 1958, p. 213. O'Brien's book is perhaps the most comprehensive and most uncompromising work in defense of the moralist position published in recent years.

23. Pius XII, "Allocution to Teaching Sisters", September 13, 1951, in Daughters of St. Paul, *Papal Teachings: Education*, translated by Aldo Rebeschini. Boston: St. Paul Editions, 1960, p. 409.

24. Pius XII, "El Especialisimo Amor", in *ibid.*, p. 483.

25. Pius XI, "Caritatem decet", March 4, 1939, in *ibid.*, pp. 193-194.

26. Pius XI, *Divini Illius Magistri*, in *ibid.*, p. 243.

27. In reckoning eight pages, the St. Paul Editions text was used. The important thing here is not the specific number of pages,

but rather that the papal text in question not only is situated in the suffusional context of a treatment of the Catholic school, but indeed is the culmination and crowning point of this treatment.

28. *Ibid.*
29. *Ibid.*, p. 239.
30. *Ibid.*, p. 237.
31. Franz de Hovre, *Catholicism in Education*, translated by Edward B. Jordan. New York: Benziger, 1934, p. 118.
32. John D. Redden and Francis A. Ryan, *A Catholic Philosophy of Education*. Milwaukee: Bruce, 1942, p. 98. Compare this with the fourth and last edition of this book (1956), p. 134, in which the same view is expressed.
33. *Ibid.*, pp. 282-286.
34. William A. Kelly, "Foreword," in Sister Barbara Zulinska, C.R., *Ad Resurrectionem: New Perspectives in Catholic Education*, translated by Sister Mary Gertrude, C.R. Trenton, N.J.: White Eagle Printing Co., 1962.
35. *Ibid.*, p. 6.
36. *Ibid.*, p. 7.
37. *Ibid.*, p. 422.
38. George A. Kelly, *The Catholic Family Handbook*. New York: Random House, 1959, p. x. Of interest is the fact that in the mid-1960s Kelly was transferred from the chancery's Family Life Bureau to the education division.
39. *Ibid.*, p. 62.
40. O'Brien, *op. cit.*, p. 167.
41. *Ibid.*, p. 53.
42. *Ibid.*, p. 184.
43. *Ibid.*, p. 175.
44. *Ibid.*, p. 202.
45. Reginald A. Neuwien, editor, *Catholic Schools in Action: A Report*. Notre Dame, Ind.: University of Notre Dame Press, 1966.
46. Interview by the present writer with Reginald A. Neuwien, June 26, 1967.
47. Neuwien's study included "14,519 students [and their parents] in the eighth and twelfth grades of 104 [Catholic] secondary schools and 218 [Catholic] elementary schools within 13 representative dioceses. The dioceses were selected as representative on the basis of geographic location, size, Catholic population, urban-suburban-rural characteristics, and potential financial resources. The schools within each diocese were a purposive

sampling representing the various important characteristics that distinguish Catholic schools". *Ibid.*, p. 157.

48. *Ibid.*, pp. 229-230.

49. *Ibid.*, p. 280. Neuwien regards table 124 on page 230 of his report as more valid than table 125 on page 281. Both data are, of course, accurate but were derived in different ways. The principal difference in the two tables occurs in the first category, "most important," in re the ranking of the importance of religious practice. The other two of the three "most important" and of the three "most successful" outcomes, viz., "honest, truthful" and "knowledge of God," are, of course, still the top two, though in reverse order in both tables.

50. Greeley and Rossi, *op. cit.*

51. The sample for the first group was drawn "from a previously existing national sample of Catholics. Precisely 2,753 Catholics between the ages of twenty-three and fifty-seven were selected for personal interviewing. In addition, 1,000 self-administered questionnaires were left at the homes of the remaining Catholic respondents of the 1962 sample who were in the proper age brackets." (*Ibid.*, p. 16). The intellectual and liberal elite, for the purposes of this investigation, were readers of the weekly Catholic periodical *The Commonweal*. A questionnaire was mailed to a randomly selected sample of 1,000 readers of this periodical.

52. *Ibid.*, p. 206. The total is greater than 100 percent because of multiple answers.

53. *Ibid.*, p. 214. The total is greater than 100 percent because of multiple answers.

54. Thomas C. Donlan, O.P., *Theology and Education*. Dubuque, Iowa: Brown, 1952, p. 58; for very much the same words, see Donlan's fellow Thomist, Herbert Johnston, *A Philosophy of Education*. New York: McGraw-Hill Catholic Series in Education, 1963.

55. *Ibid.*, p. 59.

56. Vincent Edward Smith, *The School Examined: Its Aim and Content*. Milwaukee: Bruce, 1960, p. 33 footnote, see also p. ix.

57. *Ibid.*, pp. 14-18.

58. *Ibid.*, p. 28.

59. *Ibid.*, p. 93.

60. This point constituted one of Smith's principal theses in his 1961 Delta Epsilon Sigma address.

61. McCluskey, *op. cit.*, pp. 60-61.

62. Lorenzo Reed, S.J., "Excellence for Whom," *Bulletin of the*

National Catholic Educational Association, LVII (August 1960), p. 268.

63. Johnston, *op. cit.,* p. 107.
64. Smith, *op. cit.,* pp. 33-34.
65. See, for example, Thomas Aquinas, *Eth. X,* as well as the analysis of this Thomistic text in Pierre Conway, O.P., *Principles of Education: A Thomistic Approach.* Washington, D.C.: Thomist Press, 1960, pp. 71-74.
66. McCluskey, *op. cit.,* p. 59.
67. McCluskey, *op. cit.,* p. 77.
68. Donlan, *op. cit.,* p. 73.
69. Donlan, *op. cit.,* pp. 62-63.
70. *Ibid.,* p. 76.
71. Johnston, *op. cit.,* pp. 109-110.
72. McCluskey developed this point in careful detail at his speech at the University of Dayton in the Spring of 1967.
73. This point was elaborated on by Neil McCluskey in a discussion with the present writer, July 3, 1967.
74. McCluskey, *op. cit.,* p. 60.
75. *Ibid.,* p. 74.
76. *Ibid.,* p. 73.
77. *Ibid.,* p. 78.
78. Johnston, *op. cit.,* p. 120.
79. *Ibid.*
80. Leo R. Ward, C.S.C., *New Life in Catholic Schools.* St. Louis: Herder, 1958, p. 15.
81. Pius XI, *Divini Illius Magistri, op. cit.,* p. 239.
82. *Ibid.,* p. 237.
83. Daniel Callahan, "Student Freedom" in Edward Manier and John W. Houck, editors, *Academic Freedom and the Catholic University.* Notre Dame, Ind.: Fides, 1967, p. 140.
84. Thomas O'Dea, *American Catholic Dilemma.* New York: Sheed and Ward, 1958, p. 110.
85. Ward, *op. cit.,* p. 24.
86. Pierre Teilhard de Chardin, *The Divine Milieu.* New York: Harper and Row, 1960, p. 34.
87. Emanuel Cardinal Suhard, *Growth or Decline: The Church Today,* translated by James Corbett, Notre Dame, Indiana: Fides, 1948, p. 82.
88. O'Dea, *op. cit.,* p. 111.
89. O'Brien, *op. cit.,* p. 165.
90. Walter J. Ong, S.J., "Academic Excellence and the Cosmic Vision," *Bulletin of the National Catholic Educational Associa-*

tion, LVIII (August 1960), p. 41.

91. Jacques Maritain, "On Some Typical Aspects of Christian Education," in Edmund Fuller, editor, *The Christian Idea of Education*. New Haven: Yale University Press, 1957, p. 181.

92. Teilhard de Chardin, *op. cit.*, p. 36.

93. James B. Conant, *The American High School Today*. New York: McGraw-Hill, 1959; Frank Bowles, "The Nature of Guidance," *Personnel and Guidance Journal* XXXVIII (October 1959), pp. 112-120; Frank Kerins, "No Priority for Guidance," *Catholic Educational Review*, LV (February 1957), pp. 82-88.

94. For a review of the pertinent research on this topic, see James Michael Lee and Nathaniel J. Pallone, *Guidance and Counseling in Schools: Foundations and Processes*. New York: McGraw-Hill Catholic Series in Education, 1966, pp. 414-438.

95. Most Rev. John B. McDowell, "The Encyclicals on Education and the Catholic Secondary Schools," *Bulletin of the National Catholic Educational Association*, LVI (August 1959), p. 219. Italics supplied.

96. Sister M. Judith Therese, "Realizing Our Philosophy through Literature," *Bulletin of the National Catholic Educational Association*, LII (August 1955), pp. 290-295.

97. John L. Childs, *Education and Morals*. New York: Appleton-Century-Crofts, 1950, pp. 135-154.

98. See, for example, the analysis of Paul J. Reiss, "Perspectives on American Society, Value Systems, and the Catholic Schools," *National Catholic Guidance Conference Journal*, IX (Winter 1967), p. 81.

99. The Core curriculum is a technical term. For a discussion of this concept, together with its relevance to the Catholic school, see James Michael Lee, *Principles and Methods of Secondary Education*. New York: McGraw-Hill Catholic Series in Education, 1963, especially pp. 201-208; 317-318; 491-492.

100. John E. Walsh, C.S.C., "The University and the Church," in Manier and Houck, *op. cit.*, p. 112.

101. Philip Gleason, "American Catholic Higher Education: An Historical Perspective," in Robert Hassenger, editor, *The Shape of Catholic Higher Education*. Chicago: University of Chicago Press, 1967, p. 52.

102. Understanding, knowledge, and wisdom are not defined here according to the mode of St. Thomas or of the Scholastics.

103. Allen Wheelis, *The Quest for Identity*. New York: Norton, 1958.

104. Erik H. Erikson, *Identity and the Life Cycle*. New York: International Universities Press, 1959.

105. John Dewey, *Democracy and Education*. New York: Macmillan, 1916, p. 59.
106. Johnston, *op. cit.*, p. 117.
107. McDowell, *loc. cit.*
108. *Declaration, op. cit.*, p. 643.
109. *Ibid.*, pp. 645-646.
110. One of the best accounts of the history of the Declaration is to be found in Mark Hurley, *Declaration on Christian Education of Vatican Council II: A Commentary*. Glen Rock, N. Y.: Paulist Press, 1966, pp. 26-58.
111. "Intervention" is the technical term used to denote a speech by a council Father in general debate in St. Peter's.
112. Edward L. Heston, C.S.C., "Session No. 3, News Bulletin No. 46, General Congregation No. 125," *Concilio Ecumenico Vaticano II*. Rome: Ufficio Stampa, privately duplicated and circulated November 18, 1964, p. 2.
113. Paul-Emile Cardinal Leger, quoted in Hurley, *op. cit.*, pp. 48-49.
114. Paul-Emile Cardinal Leger, quoted in Xavier Rynne, *The Third Session: The Debates and Decrees of Vatican Council II, September 14 to November 21, 1964*. New York: Farrar, Straus and Giroux, 1965, p. 226. See also Heston, *loc. cit.*, for much the same sense.
115. Heston, Session No. 3, News Bulletin No. 46 . . ., *op. cit.* p. 6.
116. In the late 1930s, a study group was commissioned by the Policies Committee to draw up a tentative draft of a statement of goals. This the group did. However, the Policies Committee rejected the draft as being too heavy and cumbersome, and hence unusable. A second draft was also rejected for the same basic reasons. A third draft was mimeographed and submitted to more than one hundred competent principals, administrators, and professors of education, both Catholic and non-Catholic, for their frank criticisms. The fourth and final draft, which resulted from this evaluative criticism, was officially presented to the Secondary School Department at the NCEA's annual convention in 1939. The following year a rather drastic revision of this statement was proposed. Two years later, still further revisions were urged. The fourth and last revision group decided in 1944 that the original 1939 statement should be accepted with certain minor changes. It is this 1944 statement which constitutes the official "Objectives." Thus it can readily be appreciated that much time, effort, and deliberation went into the evolution of this document. For accounts of revision developments, see "Report of the Policies Committee," *Bulletin*

of the National Catholic Educational Association, XLI (August 1944), pp. 234-235. See also Julian L. Maline, S.J., "Aims and Results of Catholic High Schools: A Tentative Statement of the Objectives of Secondary Education in the United States," *Catholic School Journal,* XL (December 1940), pp. 146-149.

117. *Ibid.,* p. 146.

118. Policies Committee, Secondary School Department, National Catholic Educational Association, "The Objectives of Catholic Secondary Education in the United States," *Catholic High School Quarterly Bulletin,* II (April 1944), p. 21.

119. Heston, Session No. 3, News Bulletin No. 46 . . ., *op. cit.,* pp. 4-5.

120. James C. Donohue, "A New Vision for Catholic Education," *Bulletin of the National Catholic Educational Association,* LXIII (August 1966), pp. 285-286.

Designed, produced and distributed by Geo. A. Pflaum, Publisher, Inc.

General Editor: Russell Shaw, Director of Editorial Services, National Catholic Educational Association

NCEA Papers: *No. 1 The Parish School Board, by*
Rev. Olin J. Murdick
No. 2 Team Teaching: A Rationale, by
Melvin P. Heller, D.Ed.
No. 3 The Purpose of Catholic Schooling, by
James Michael Lee

Subscriptions to NCEA Papers (five titles, bimonthly, September through May) are obtainable at $7.50 per subscription. Copies of individual titles are available at $1.50 per copy. Discounts on quantity orders of individual titles are: 10 percent on 7-13 copies; 20 percent on 14 or more copies. On orders of less than $5.00 not accompanied by payment, a 45-cent postage-handling charge will be added. Make checks payable to:

National Catholic Educational Association
NCEA Papers, Box 667, Dayton, Ohio 45401